by
June Rayfield Welch

Dallas   •   G.L.A. Press   •   1975

Copyright 1975
by
June Rayfield Welch

Library of Congress Catalog Card No.
75-39538

ISBN 0-912854-07-7

First Printing November 1975

Published by
G.L.A. Press
Dallas, Texas

Printed by

Waco, Texas

Dedication

For old buddy Jason, and for those folks who settled the Plains...

including Uncle Sam Burrow, who looked after Charlie Goodnight's buffalo,

and those cowhands and their ladies who danced on wagon sheets beside the neighborhood tree.

The Author

June Rayfield Welch has degrees from Texas Christian University, the University of Texas at Arlington, Texas Tech University and George Washington University. He practiced law prior to becoming Academic Dean of the University of Dallas where he is presently chairman of the department of history. His books include: A FAMILY HISTORY; THE TEXAS COURTHOUSE; TEXAS: NEW PERSPECTIVES; HISTORIC SITES OF TEXAS; DAVE'S TUNE, a novel; PEOPLE AND PLACES IN THE TEXAS PAST; and the novel, AND HERE'S TO CHARLEY BOYD.

Introduction

As the nation celebrates its bicentennial, civilization on the High Plains of Texas will be only one hundred years old and the people of Ysleta and Socorro will have spent nearly three centuries at the Pass of the North. In early 1876 the Panhandle was unsettled, and the country between Weatherford and El Paso remained as sparsely populated as it had been before the withdrawal of the Comanche; a few months earlier Quanah Parker had led his Quahadi band—the last hostiles still at large—onto the reservation north of Red River. At last the Comanchería was open to settlement; near the close of 1876, almost 200 years after refugees from the Indian rebellion in New Mexico settled below present El Paso, Casimero Romero, Charles Goodnight, and Thomas Bugbee moved into the empty Panhandle.

All things considered, this past summer seemed an appropriate time to visit these newest and oldest sections of the state. I decided I owed myself a few trips to the extreme west and north of Texas, for they are special places. No matter how often one goes to El Paso he is surprised and pleased by the vigor and beauty of that valley, where the settlers considered their river to be more than a watering place for stock and a source of timber. The Río Grande was the artery nourishing that country of scanty rainfall; its waters, directed through irrigation ditches, made the land yield whatever was required by those who sojourned there. This differed from my Cooke County experience in which the creeks and Red River were mainly impediments to travel and transport, requiring bridging, subject to overflow, and held in the affections of small boys and other sportsmen of cane-pole and cork-bobber class. Early visitors to Paso del Norte—such as discoverer of peaks Lt. Zebulon Pike—admired the orchards and vineyards and fields and the perpetual summer and song of the valley.

On the other hand, the High Plains provoked little extravagant favorable comment. While the Panhandle held a powerful attraction for me, its reputation promised only a harsh climate—"ain't nuthin between Amarillo and the North Pole but a bobwire fence, and it's on the ground"—and a proud future for those foolish enough to go there and tough enough to stay. My connections with the Plains country were personal. Stories of cousins, never met, who cowboyed there long ago, and any number of short journeys made when I was recently admitted to the practice of law in Lubbock, drew me to that flat country.

Uncle Sam Burrow, of Armstrong County, had been one of Charlie Goodnight's hands; my mother owned photographs of him tending the old man's buffalo herd. And Uncle Johnny Welch, the only one of my grandfather's brothers to choose the Plains, moved his family to Briscoe County in 1899. In the canyons he felled trees and packed out—by burro—posts and firewood. Aunt Docia had to chop the tough, virgin soil with a hatchet to loosen it sufficiently to accomodate a garden. Late one afternoon, while building their dugout—they had four children then, and seven were yet to come—Uncle Johnny rummaged through his pockets and discovered he had only 15¢ in all the world. Because it was so wildly ridiculous to be so broke while starting a new life in such an improbable place he and Aunt Docia could not stop laughing, and they sprawled upon the open prairie, overcome by mirth. In the end Uncle Johnny owned more land and stock than his brothers and sisters put together.

Perhaps because it was the most recent frontier, or maybe on account of the kind of people who settled there, the Panhandle produced an open, friendly, free-wheeling, independent kind of human—a Texan-type Texan. Until a generation ago they wore runover boots and big hats—some still do—and made their wives get out and open the barbed wire gates for their pickup trucks en route to town on a Saturday.

The Plains country will always exert its pull on one who has lived there, and my son was born in Lubbock. The research and photography for parts of this book provided a welcome excuse for responding to that insistent summons to the land of Thomas Cree's little tree, where wind and sand will cut the shine off an automobile bumper, where the water gives children strong—if sometimes mottled—teeth, and the gash of the Palo Duro in that level land still appears suddenly and without warning, and everyone owns a pickup truck and waves at you.

I am obligated to the Institute of Texan Cultures; Foote, Cone and Belding; the Oklahoma Historical Society; the Western History Collections of the University of Oklahoma Library; the Smithsonian Institution; the Panhandle-Plains Historical Museum; the U. S. Information Agency; the Library of Congress; Galveston's Rosenberg Library; Fort Worth's Amon Carter Museum; the Library of Texas A & M University; the *Waco Tribune; The Cattleman;* the El Paso Public Library; the *Corpus Christi Caller-Times;* the Denver Public Library; the Abell-Hanger Foundation, the War Department General Staff; the Office of War Information; the National Archives; the Masonic Home and School; John A. Cypher, Jr., of the King Ranch; and Mrs. John Kenedy, Jr., of the Kenedy Ranch, for their generosity in permitting the use of photographs. Raff Frano bettered my camera work by his fine developing and printing. Sister Ruth Quatman of the University of Dallas Library located and obtained dozens of books. Lynn Guier drew old Ben Milam and the maps, and Joan and Nick Curtis designed the dust jacket. Sister Frances Marie Manning gave the manuscript a couple of critical readings and tried—once more—to improve my use of the language. Bill Shirley, Mike Prim, Lane Price, Linda Stanford, and others at Texian Press were efficient and helpful. And my good secretary, Kathryn Pokladnik, performed in her customary (extraordinary) fashion in putting the manuscript into shape and preparing the index and bibliography. To all of these good friends—as well as to Don Cowan and the University—I am beholden.

June R. Welch
University of Dallas
October 21, 1975

Table of Contents

THE GLORY THAT WAS TEXAS

by
June Rayfield Welch

A New Mexico Rebellion Peopled the Pass of the North

Most of the handful of Spaniards who had entered the empty country above present Chihuahua had followed the Río Conchos to the vicinity of present Presidio and then proceeded up the Río Grande, but Don Juan Oñate—who made the first permanent Spanish settlement in New Mexico—traveled a more direct route to the Great River of the North. For many years Spain had kept settlers out of that country, but Oñate was one of the most influential men in New Spain; his wife was Cortés' granddaughter and Montezuma's great-granddaughter. On April 30, 1598, about 15 miles below present Juárez—and after a mass and the performance of a play written for the occasion—Oñate proclaimed, "in the name of the most Christian king, Don Philip, our lord,...and in the name of the crown of Castile...I take possession of...the lands of the said Río del Norte...."

When the Spaniards began searching for a good place to cross the river, some Manso Indians showed them a ford that had been used for generations by those making their way through the mountains; calling it El Paso del Norte, Oñate took his huge expedition into New Mexico through this Pass of the North. The train of 83 wagons and carts—and thousands of sheep, goats, cattle and horses—was four miles long. The 400 accompanying him included 11 Franciscans and 130 married men who were bringing their families. High on the Río Grande Oñate chose as his capital the Tewa pueblo of Ohke, which he renamed San Juan de los Caballeros. His successor moved the capital 25 miles to the southeast, where he founded La Villa Real de la Santa Fé de San Francisco—or simply Santa Fé—in 1610. Every third year the royal caravans brought supplies to the colony, following the King's Highway through the Pass of the North; it was not long before some travelers realized that good crossing of the Río Grande was an appropriate place for a mission and settlement.

In 1659, after unsuccessful attempts by others, Father García de San Francisco came down from Socorro mission, chose a site south of the ford in present Juárez, founded the Mission Nuestra Señora de Guadalupe del Paso, and built a church of mud and sticks for the Manso Indians. A few Spaniards settled there, and a community developed which was usually called Paso del Norte. By 1668—when a new church was completed—the population was about a thousand, mostly Indians and mixed bloods tilling the soil. Visitors praised the fruit and wine and looked forward to stopping at Paso del Norte. Many Indians had become Christians but still were not fully accustomed to the new religion; other Indians were quite hostile toward the Spaniards. But the unrest at the Pass was much less serious than that existing in New Mexico, where several attempts at rebellion had failed by 1675. The Indians had been exploited by settlers and Franciscans, who tried to make Europeans of them. Attempting to suppress native religious observances, a New Mexico governor charged 47 medicine men with witchcraft and sorcery, hanged three or four, and punished the others; this antag-

Manso Indians showed Don Juan Oñate an ancient fording place across the Río Grande; it was situated along the northernmost passage through the mountains remaining free of ice and snow throughout the year. Oñate called it the Pass of the North.

onized the Indians, who were contented Christians only so long as witch doctors were available to provide protection from evil spirits.

One of the chastized medicine men, Popé, began planning the destruction of the Europeans, who numbered about 2,800. Most of the Spaniards occupied haciendas south of present Albuquerque, and the rest lived in or near Santa Fé, the only Spanish town north of Mexico except for the one at the Pass of the North. Mainly the Spaniards were ranchers and farmers, but there were also a few soldiers and 32 Franciscan missionaries who served 16,000 Christianized pueblo Indians.

After five years of planning, Popé was ready to precipitate a general revolt in which all the Spanish would be killed; those escaping New Mexico would be slaughtered by the Manso at the Pass. Their estates would be looted, the churches destroyed, and the Indians could return to the old ways. The plot was discovered two days before the insurrection was to begin, so Popé, from the Tigua pueblo of Taos, ordered an immediate attack. On August 10, 1680, the rebels struck. Some 400 men, women, and children were massacred. About 1,500 southern New Mexico settlers found refuge at the Tigua pueblo and Spanish convent of Isleta, below present Albuquerque. Isleta's 2,000 Indians had not taken part in the uprising. From Isleta the Spaniards fled southward and were joined by Governor Antonio de Otermín and survivors from the Santa Fé area.

The refugees reached La Salineta, within present Texas and about four leagues above Paso del Norte, on September 29. Anxious to have the river between themselves and the rebellious Indians, they crossed the Río Grande and stopped at Paso del Norte. In spite of the governor's orders many settlers had continued on to Mexico, so there remained only about 2,000 refugees, including 155 men able to fight and 317 Indians of both sexes and all ages. The small community was unable to accommodate the expanded population, even though the New Mexicans were to remain only until they could return home. In October Otermín, deciding against an immediate re-entry, settled his charges into three camps along the Río Grande. Below Paso del Norte was the Real del Santísimo Sacramento and, two leagues farther, the Real de San Pedro de Alcántara. The last encampment was San Lorenzo—Otermín's headquarters—in the neighborhood of that bivouac where Oñate had taken possession of all land drained by the Rio Grande nearly a century before.

The governor asked that a presidio be established at the Pass for protection from the New Mexico rebels; in January, 1681, the Viceroy granted the request and authorized a garrison of 50 soldiers. That November Otermín took 146 badly equipped troops and 112 Indians into New Mexico to punish the rebels and restore Spanish rule. The campaign was a failure, and when he returned in February, 1682, he brought 385 Tigua Indians from Isleta to keep them from resuming their old practices and to help convert the Manso. The newcomers aggravated the critical overpopulation problem. Now long term plans had to be made, for the prospects of an early recovery of New Mexico were slight. Within a few months three Spanish and six Indian settlements had come into being. Otermín's plan to consolidate the refugees into three towns was approved by the Viceroy, but Indians, for their own protection, were to be segregated from the Spanish. Although deserting the area was a treasonable offense punishable by death, in the fall of 1682 only 40 Spaniards remained at Paso del Norte and 80 at San Lorenzo.

An obelisk and a bust of Francisco Madero mark the Mexican side of the international boundary at the Pass, Madero succeeded long-time dictator Porfiro Diaz and was president only a short time before he was assassinated.

There was much privation, and the settlements were almost defenseless. Individuals had traded all they owned for food; the garrison consisted of only 19 soldiers, and none of the 72 able-bodied men had a weapon.

Don Domingo Jironza Petriz de Cruzate, who succeeded Otermín in 1683, located Presidio de Nuestra Señora del Pilar y Glorioso Señor San José near the Guadalupe mission, and because of Indian unrest the settlements were moved nearer the Pass for better protection. In the meantime Popé ruled his people from Santa Fé, where the roof of the church was gone and the walls were used as a corral for cattle. Part of the governor's palace had been destroyed and the rest turned into a pueblo. Popé died before the return of the Spanish; he and his successor were as tyrannical as the Europeans had been. The federation that made possible the Spanish expulsion dissolved, and the pueblos became self-governing. Without the Spaniards to defend them the pueblos were so vulnerable to Apache raids that many had to be abandoned.

Finally, a new governor recovered New Mexico. The wealthy Don Diego de Vargas Zapata y Luján Ponce de Leon reached Paso del Norte in February, 1691, and found the populace naked and hungry. After waging a successful local Indian campaign and establishing order—mainly at his own expense—in August, 1692, he invaded New Mexico. Instead of using the traditional approach of threats and force Vargas offered peace and absolution; by the year's end 23 pueblos had been recovered without a fight and 2,000 Indians had been baptized. As the Spaniards were returning to Paso del Norte they were attacked by a band of Apache. A captured warrior admitted stealing Spanish horses; Vargas informed him of the penalty and advised him to become a Christian before his execution. A friar baptized the Apache, naming him Agustin, and Vargas "ordered the lieutenant of cavalry to have four soldiers take the Indian off to the side and shoot him forthwith, giving him a good death."

On October 4, 1693, Vargas set out to reoccupy New Mexico, taking 100 soldiers, 70 families, 18 friars, and some Indians from the Pass. After some fighting—during the intervening year most of the Indians had changed their minds about the Spaniards' return—Spain once more held New Mexico. Anne Hughes noted that:

> The importance of El Paso (Juárez) in the frontier history of New Spain can scarcely be overestimated. At the most critical period in the early history of New Mexico, El Paso (Juárez) became the bulwark of the New Mexican colonists against the ravages of the Pueblo Indians and made it possible eventually for Spanish arms to repossess the abandoned province....Though the beginning of Texas is commonly associated with a small group of missions established by Massanet in 1690 on the Neches River in Eastern Texas, as a matter of fact, the true beginnings of what is now Texas are to be found in the settlements grouped along the Rio del Norte in the El Paso District.

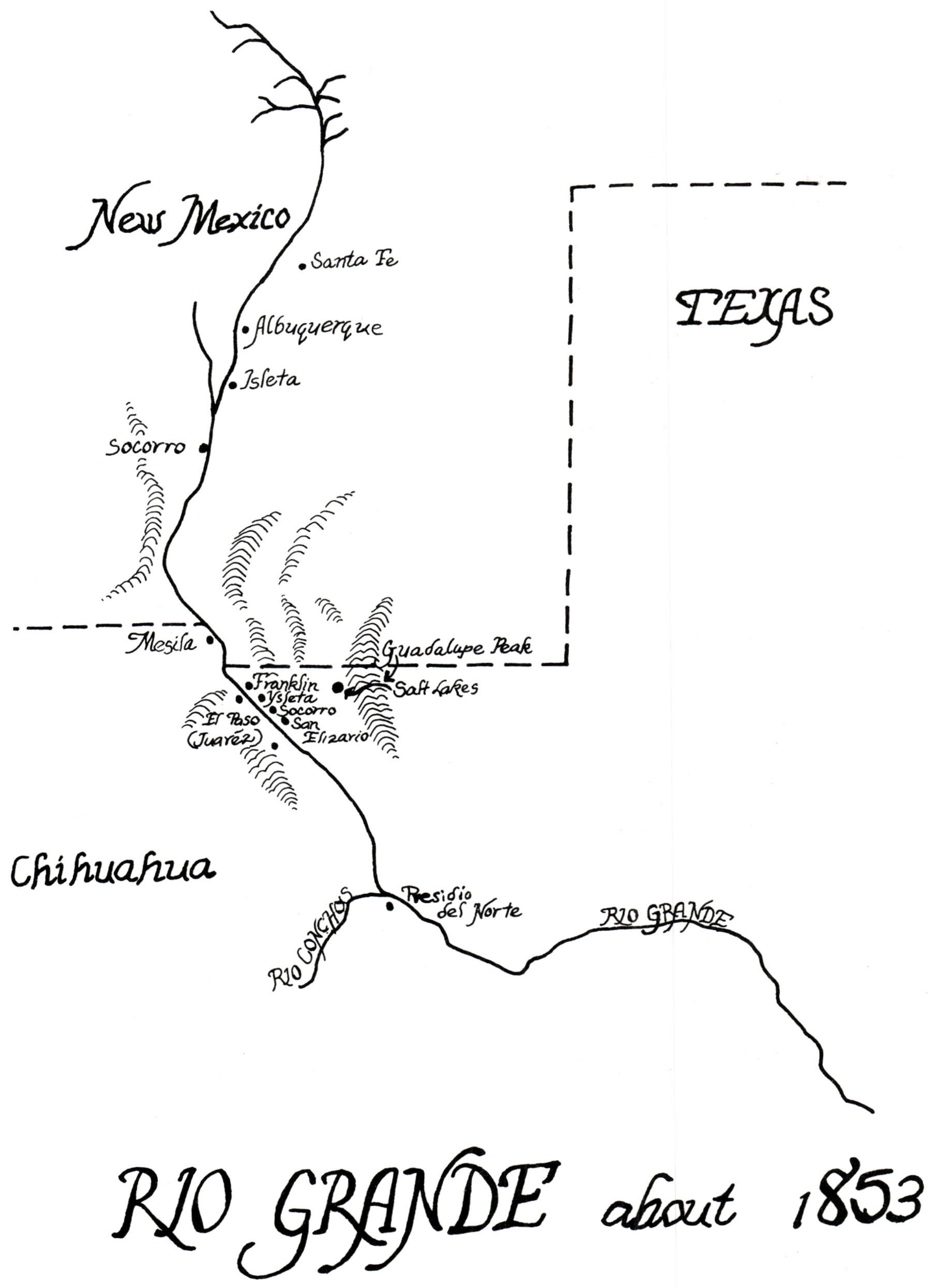

New Mexico
Santa Fe
Albuquerque
Isleta
Socorro
Mesila
Franklin
Ysleta
Socorro
El Paso
(Juarez)
San
Elizario
Guadalupe Peak
Salt Lakes
TEXAS
Chihuahua
Presidio del Norte
RIO CONCHOS
RIO GRANDE
RIO GRANDE about 1853

Ysleta Is the Oldest Town in Texas

In 1680 Governor Antonio de Otermín halted his 2,000 New Mexico refugees south of the Río Grande. The Spaniards and 317 Piro and Tigua Indians from the pueblos of Socorro, Senecú, Sevilleta, Alamillo, and Isleta were settled in three camps along the river. Returning from his fruitless campaign to recover New Mexico, in 1682, Otermín brought 385 more Indians from Isleta pueblo, which he had burned. The Isletans had become Christians again, and because the rebels might persecute them Otermín intended to settle them with the Tigua at Santísimo Sacramento. Otermín's failure meant that the refugees would need more permanent quarters. After inspecting the valley Otermín concluded that the sites of the three Spanish villages and six Indian pueblos which had evolved were the best available; other possible locations were either too far above the river for irrigation or so low as to be subject to flooding. In February, 1682, San Lorenzo, the headquarters of the governor, the cabildo of Santa Fé, and the other Spaniards, was relocated about 12 leagues from Paso del Norte. The Piro and Tompiro were at the pueblo of Senecú, the Tigua were at Corpus Christi de la Isleta—which was probably the same site earlier called Santísimo Sacramento—and the Piro, Jemez and Tano were at the pueblo of Nuestra Señora del Socorro; the missions at Socorro and Isleta probably date from that same year. During the 1936 Texas Centennial it was noted that four acres at Ysleta had been regularly cultivated for more than 250 years.

The new residents of the valley, frustrated in their desire to go home, were experiencing a severe drouth. The soil and climate were not to their liking, and the Apache and other hostiles harrassed them. They dug roots to stay alive and complained of having no clothing to wear to mass; men were without trousers and weapons, having bartered everything for food. In March, 1684, the Manso and other local tribes revolted, suggesting the wisdom of moving the communities closer to the presidio. In spite of Spanish protests—and they had lived so far apart in New Mexico that Santa Fé, the only town, had just a few hundred people—the settlements were concentrated. In late 1684 a census showed Isleta's population to be 198; San Lorenzo had 354 residents, and Paso del Norte had 499. Therefore, there were only 1051 citizens in the valley, slightly more than half the number which had arrived with Otermín four years before.

The Isleta site was an island formed by the splitting of the Río Grande into two channels; perhaps by coincidence the New Mexico mission and pueblo had been similarly situated, Isleta's name meant "little island." The old Isleta mission had been founded in 1621 for the 2,000 Tigua who lived there; the New Mexico Pueblo Indians were of three linguistic groups: Zunian, Keresan, and Tanoan. The largest family, the Tanoan, was composed of the Tewa, the Piro, the Tano, the Jemez, and the Tigua.

The first church at Corpus Christi de Isleta, or Isleta del Sur, was probably built of logs on the island's high ground, which afforded a good view of the

Tigua Indians settled at this place, Ysleta, El Paso County, Texas, after the New Mexico rebellion of 1680.

countryside. Settlers used the church as a place of safety from marauding Indians. Governor Vargas granted the church, convent and land of the mission to the Franciscans shortly before he left for New Mexico in 1692. Although Vargas wrote that the Tigua lived in "some miserable huts in the pueblo of Isleta, in the district of El Paso and so it will be desirable to restore them to their pueblo," there is no record that any of them returned to New Mexico then; later some did go; they helped rebuild the pueblo on its old site about 1716. But most of the Tigua remained at Isleta del Sur.

A new church, San Antonío de los Tiguas de Isleta was completed in 1744; later it became Nuestra Señora de Carmen. The statue of the patron saint—brought from New Mexico in 1680—and other ancient furnishings were destroyed in 1907 when the roof and interior burned as sulphur candles were being used to rid the church of bats. The present church retains the six-foot-thick walls of the old structure. The Franciscans withdrew in 1852 after 172 years, and in 1881 the Jesuits took charge and changed the name to Our Lady of Mount Carmel.

Although most of the Spaniards returned to New Mexico, the Indians did not. In 1751 King Charles V of Spain granted title to the lands of Isleta del Sur; the pueblo of San Antonio de Isleta received that tract extending one league north, south, east and west of the church, part of which Ysleta, Texas occupies now. When the bishop of Durango was there in 1760, the population of 560 included 429 Indians. Ysleta, the seat of El Paso County between 1880 and 1884, had about 10,000 residents in 1940; it is now within the limits of the City of El Paso.

The Tigua have always had a tribal government, which presently functions under the leadership of descendants of those refugees of three centuries ago. While working for a Captain Baylor in January 1881, three Tigua scouts killed some Apache warriors; the event was the occasion for the last scalp dance at Ysleta, a celebration which lasted three days and nights. To preserve their most important institutions, in 1895 the Tigua adopted a constitution and by laws. The first item bound the Tigua of Ysleta del Sur (Ysleta of the South) to celebrate the festival of Saint Anthony; this referred to ancient resentments over the attempted replacement of their patron, San Antonio; in the 1680's several hundred Tigua threatened to found another community where they might venerate Saint Anthony until the authorities compromised and designated San Antonio as one of the community's two patron saints. By the constitution the Tigua agreed to submit to rules and punishments decreed by tribal authorities in addition to the laws of Texas and the United States. The officers included a Cacique Mayor, who was to convene a council each year for the election of the governor, lieutenant governor and subordinate officers whose main concern was with preserving the traditional dances and religious observances and combatting witchcraft. The Tigua Indians in El Paso County in February, 1970, numbered 409; 58% were less than 21 years old. While retaining old beliefs and customs the Tigua have lost much of their language and speak a dialect composed of Spanish, English and Indian words.

The mission church at Ysleta, erected in 1744, was partially destroyed by fire in 1907 and was rebuilt, using the old walls. Ancient furnishings brought from New Mexico in 1680 were lost in the conflagration.

The Tigua Indians of Ysleta bake bread in ovens such as they have used for hundreds of years.

The Tigua have constructed new pueblo buildings at Ysleta for use in demonstrating their ancient crafts and way of life.

San Miguel Chose the Site of Socorro

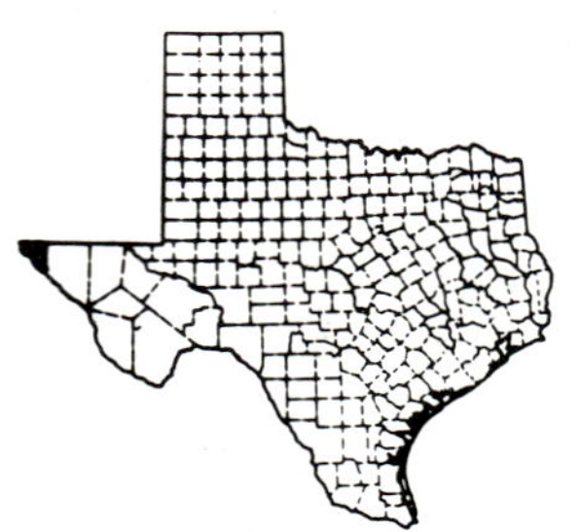

In 1598 Oñate, after crossing the Río Grande at the Pass of the North, traversed the harsh Dead Man's March and found Piro pueblos on both sides of the river. The people of the third village, Teipana, welcomed the Spaniards with gifts of grain. Oñate called the town Socorro because of this aid or succor, and across the river at Pilabo he erected a mission building that burned a few years later and was supplanted by the Mission Nuestra Señora del Socorro.

In 1680 Governor Antonio de Otermín, retreating from New Mexico, brought 317 Indians to the Pass of the North. The Piro from Socorro mission camped at San Pedro de Alcántara. Otermín invaded New Mexico in 1681 and, upon realizing that a reconquest was then impossible, burned the deserted Socorro mission. Socorro was not re-established until about 1817; it occupies the old Pilabo pueblo site; a wall of the existing church of San Miguel may be a remnant of the 1598 mission.

Upon Otermín's return from New Mexico the mission Nuestra Señora de Socorro was founded for the Piro, Tano, and Jemez Indians. Because some neophytes conspired to kill Fray Antonio Guerra, in 1693 Socorro was moved to within a league of Isleta. The plotters fled to New Mexico.

Governor Vargas granted the land and buildings of the Socorro mission to the Franciscans a few weeks before he reconquered New Mexico. The conveyance was accomplished on May 20, 1692, in good form, with the governor and priest entering the church, and the Franciscan accepting the grant orally and by actions; he walked on the steps of the altar, moved some of the furnishings about, inspected the premises, and acted in such manner as to demonstrate possession and dominion over the premises. In October, 1693, Vargas took 800 people—including 70 families and some friendly Indians—north for resettlement. Most of the Spaniards, but only a few of the Indians, returned to New Mexico, leaving behind five small pueblos: Isleta, Senecú, Socorro, San Lorenzo and Paso del Norte. Socorro was on a large island—about 20 miles long and four to six miles wide—with Isleta; the erratic Río Grande moved them from the north to the south bank and back any number of times; a change in the channel about 1831 left them (and San Elizario) on the Texas side.

The land occupied by the Socorro pueblo was granted later, perhaps in 1751; about 50 families lived at Socorro then. The church building, half a mile from the present site, was destroyed by flood in 1829. Local legend holds that the current location was selected by the patron saint; a statue of St. Michael was being moved to New Mexico by ox cart when the wheels became stuck and could not be moved. This was interpreted as an order that the image remain there. The church, La Purísima, was built at that place—where the statue may still be seen—and is called San Miguel by many. A few rafters from the original church were used in the ceiling of this one, and they probably constitute the oldest relics of Christianity in Texas.

According to Nicholas Lafora, in 1766 there was a continuous settlement seven leagues long and with a population of 5,000 on the Río Grande. He wrote:

> All this stretch of land is well-cultivated, producing everything that is
> planted, particularly very good grapes which are in no way inferior to those

The Catholic exhibit at the 1936 Texas Centennial was modeled after the old church at Socorro, El Paso County.

of Spain. There are many European fruits which are produced in such abundance that they are allowed to rot on the trees. The inhabitants make passable wine and better brandy, but at times they do not harvest enough maize for their support, because the ground is devoted to vines and other crops.

The Catholic exhibits at the 1936 Texas Centennial in Dallas were housed in a replica of the Socorro mission.

This photograph of the interior of the Socorro church shows hand-hewn beams, some of which were used in the original mission church about 300 years ago.

Local legend teaches that the cart transporting this statue of San Miguel to New Mexico became stuck and could not be moved. This was taken as a sign that the Socorro church was to be built there.

The town of Socorro grew up around the mission settlement of Indian refugees from the New Mexico rebellion of 1680.

San Elizario Was the Biggest Town in West Texas

San Elizario was originally the Hacienda de los Tiburcios, a settlement which came into existence after Ysleta and Socorro but prior to 1760; it was situated on the same island as the mission towns; the island was finally deposited on the Texas side by a change in the river channel. The San Elizario presidio, then located in the El Porvenir area, was moved to Tiburcios in 1780 to afford Indian protection to the settlements near the Pass. The presidio's small payroll stimulated the local economy, and San Elizario was soon second in population to Paso del Norte. The presidio remained at San Elizario until about 1814, and later troops were stationed there from time to time. The fort covered about 8 acres and was enclosed by high, thick walls.

When El Paso County was organized, in 1850, San Elizario became the county seat. Its population of 1200 was six times that of El Paso, and San Elizario was the biggest town in West Texas. County government was moved to Magoffinsville in 1854 but was soon returned to San Elizario until 1866, when Ysleta was the county seat for two years. During the decade beginning in 1873 Ysleta served as the county capital, and was succeeded by El Paso in 1883.

The trade route between the Mexicos came through San Elizario. Lt. Zebulon Pike, who had been exploring the country and naming Colorado peaks was captured in 1807 by the Spaniards and brought to San Elizario on the way to Chihuahua. Pike wrote that the presidio commander's wife and sister entertained him in fine style.

California-bound goldseekers passing through San Elizario were amazed to find that "trees loaded with fruit might be seen in every garden and baskets of the same at nearly every door." Mentioning the corn, wheat, beans, vegetables and wine one traveler claimed it "makes one almost feel that he has been transported to the bowers of Eden." Another noted that in 1846 between Paso del Norte, at the head of the valley, and San Elizario, at the bottom, was a continuous line of adobe houses with their plots of gardens and vineyards. Farms seldom had more than 20 acres. Cottonwoods, to a depth of 100 yards, grew along both sides of the river.

The original church at San Elizario was destroyed by flood. An American soldier wrote that the church was located inside the walls of the old presidio; it was well furnished but "on the gold and tinsel order." Pike described a religious service there in which "all the troops attended under arms; at one part of their mass they present arms, sink on one knee, and rest the muzzle on the ground in signification of their submission to their divine master...." After the presidio chapel was lost another was built by Father Antonio Borajo in 1853. The present church was constructed in 1874.

San Elizario was badly damaged by the Salt War; people who would have contributed to its development moved away or did not settle there. When the railroad passed it by and built into El Paso, San Elizario's decline was accelerated.

The old church at San Elizario is the successor of an 18th century Spanish presidio chapel.

This San Elizario house is thought to have been occupied by the viceroy, which is impossible since he remained in Mexico City; however, the house may be, as claimed, the oldest building in Texas. Settlement began in the neighborhood by 1700; some residents claim descent from Cortés' captains who allegedly settled at San Elizario soon after the conquest of Mexico, about 1525.

The buildings on its main street reflect the age and character of San Elizario, but pantsuits sometimes replace dresses, and ponies substitute for burros.

The San Sabá Mission Was Established for the Apache

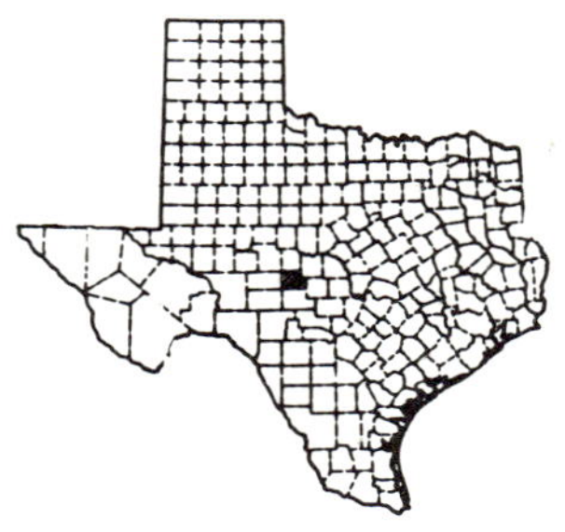

The fierce Apache had always been troublesome to the Spaniards and to other Indians. Fray Francisco Hidalgo, who had established the first mission in East Texas, had urged the founding of missions to civilize the Apache, but not until 1756 was this undertaken; in the meantime their raids took a heavy toll of Spaniards and mission Indians in Texas, New Mexico, Coahuila, and other Mexican states. It was not until the Comanche began pressing them on the north and west that the Apache showed any interest in receiving missionaries. The Comanche, having become superb horsemen, were forcing them out of the High Plains, and the Apache were seeking an ally by pretending to desire Christianity. As a result, in late 1749, a quarter-century after Fray Hidalgo had suggested missions for them, Apache representatives came to San Antonio—a place they had always terrorized—for a peace ceremony: the burial of the hatchet. In preparation for the council a great hole had been dug in the plaza. Six arrows, a lance, a tomahawk and a live horse—weapons of war—were buried, signifying the new order.

While the authorities in Texas and Mexico tried to decide whether a mission should be opened for the Apache and, if so, where it should be situated, Fray Alonso Giraldo de Terreros founded a short-lived Apache mission in Coahuila. During that same time the San Xavier missions on the San Gabriel River in Texas were failing, and the soldiers and priests and church furniture and equipment might be available should a new mission materialize. Don Pedro Romero de Terreros—because of the persuasion of his cousin, Fray Alonso—agreed to pay the expense of founding and maintaining, for three years, Apache missions in Texas. The new hundred-soldier presidio, commanded by Colonel Diego Ortiz Parrilla, would protect San Antonio from the Apache while Fray Alonso civilized them.

A decision in favor of the missions having been made, the soldiers and priests reached the vicinity of present Menard in April, 1757. The building of the first log mission, on the south side of the San Sabá River, was begun while Parrilla constructed presidio San Luis de los Amarillas, three miles away on the north bank. The priests insisted upon shielding the neophyte Indians from the corrupting influence of the soldiers, but the distance between the two sites would make it hard for the troops to protect the mission. The mission buildings—a chapel and living quarters for priests, personnel, and neophytes—were enclosed by a stockade.

Although the Apache had promised to congregate at the mission, not one appeared, disappointing the priests but confirming Parrilla's distrust of their intentions. When several thousand Apache passed through the neighborhood in June, they agreed to return after they fought the North Texas Indians. The promise was not kept. The Apache never did congregate at the mission, although they made their enemies believe the Spaniards were their allies. Therefore, the Spanish, without any influence or control over the Apache, incurred the hostility of the northern tribes. Parilla wrote the viceroy urging abandonment of the project, and the priests were dispirited.

For several weeks it was rumored that North Texas tribes planned to attack

Only a Texas Centennial marker serves as a reminder of the existence of the San Sabá
Mission.

the mission. By February of 1758 many bands of Indians were camped nearby and making regular raids on the Spaniards' livestock. More than 300 people lived at the presidio, including 237 women and children who were mainly dependents of the soldiers. Since the priests refused to come to the presidio, Parrilla stationed eight soldiers at the mission to guard the three Franciscans and two dozen servants and San Antonio mission Indians.

In the early morning of March 16, as Father Santiesteban was saying his mass, the hostile Indians attacked. At the river they whipped two Spaniards, and they wounded another as they approached the mission firing their weapons and shouting. The attackers stopped at the closed gate, stating that they came in friendship looking for Apache. They were Comanche, Bidai, Tejas, Tonkawa, and others, most in war paint; Fray Molina estimated their number at 2,000. While the leaders stressed their peaceful intentions—which Fray Terreros apparently believed—several hundred Indians poured into the stockaded mission and began taking everything of value. Armed with muskets, swords and lances the Indians killed everyone in sight. Father Terreros was shot off his horse, and Father Santiesteban was slain and decapitated before the altar. Eight others, including two scouts sent from the presidio to see what was happening, were killed.

Parrilla had fewer than fifty soldiers; the rest of the garrison was detailed elsewhere. The Indians surrounded the presidio but did not attack. On March 18 they began to leave. There followed a period of extreme privation for the Spanish. The Indians had taken or destroyed all the cattle, and the Spaniards remained inside the stockades fearing that they might return.

Fray Francisco Aparicio requested the abandonment of the mission, believing the Apache to be incorrigible. They had never come to the mission and certainly would not do so now that their enemies had attacked in such strength. Nevertheless, new priests were assigned to San Sabá, including Father Junipero Serra and Father Antonio Palou, but because Parrilla was away on a punitive expedition against the northern tribes the priests would have to await his return before going on to the mission. Instead Father Serra was ordered to California, where he established the missions which became the great cities of that state, and Father Palou chronicled those achievements.

MISSIONS OF SPANISH TEXAS

The San Sabá Presidio Protected San Antonio

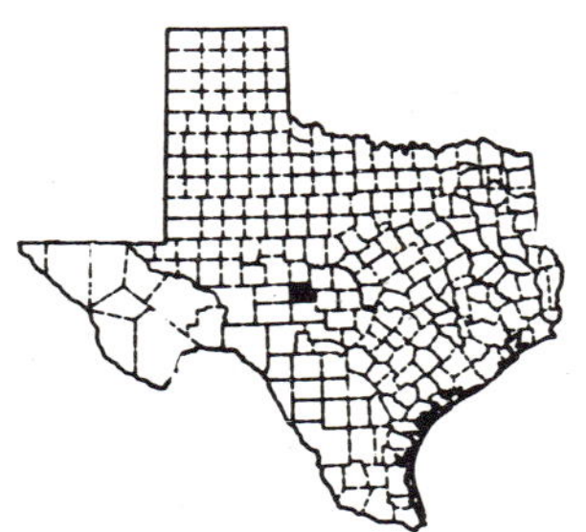

The building of Mission San Sabá de la Santa Cruz was a serious mistake. The Apache were not interested in Christianity or civilization, and the Spanish attempt to educate and convert them resulted in the massacre of March 16, 1758, and the disastrous defeat of Parrilla's expedition by the northern tribes in the following year. But the Presidio de San Luis de las Amarillas did afford protection to San Antonio—the only substantial settlement in Texas—and to settlers on the lower Río Grande.

In October, 1760, not long after his defeat at Spanish Fort, Parrilla was succeeded by Captain Felipe Rábago y Terán. Oddly, although his career had been consistently marked by incompetence and lack of character, Rábago was given command of this largest and most important presidio in Texas. Rábago erected a stone stockade—with quarters built into the walls—a blockhouse, and a moat to take the place of the wooden fort; he called it the Real Presidio de San Sabá. Rábago was instructed to establish a mission nearby, but since the Apache were apprehensive because of the massacre he agreed to a Nueces River site more than a hundred miles away; there, in January, 1762, was founded Mission San Lorenzo del Cañon. Ten miles away the priests established Mission Nuestra Señora de la Candelaria. From these missions the Apache—called "the proven enemies of humanity" by Father Morfi— "would go out to rob and kill the Indians of the north, taking with them a number of hats and other things worn by our soldiers, all of which they artfully left along the way, as if by carelessness, in order to convince that the Spaniards were the perpetrators of the crimes. At the same time they would provide themselves with arrows and shoes of the kind used by their enemies and would then commit depredations near Spanish presidios and missions where it was thought the Indians of the North were responsible." These tactics provoked the enemies of the Apache into regular attacks on the presidio, which had been weakened by the assignment of a third of its men to the Apache missions.

When the Marquis de Rubí inspected the frontier in 1767 he found two priests and no neophytes at San Lorenzo, and the Candelaria mission was abandoned. The presidio was undermanned and mismanaged, and the soldiers were held there by heavy debts owed to Rábago because of the high prices he charged for the goods he sold. Guns were not of uniform caliber, only half the soldiers had pistols, and all of the arms and equipment were poorly maintained. Declaring the presidio to be of no value—in fact, the worst in the kingdom—Rubí urged that it be razed.

The presidio was abandoned in 1770. Robert Weddle wrote in his fine book, *The San Sabá Mission*, "The stone walls and buildings had not been leveled before the presidio garrison withdrew. That remained to be done almost a century later by another generation of pioneers, badly in need of building stone with which to raise a town on the opposite bank of the San Sabá." A replica was constructed in 1936 using some of the original stone; the ruins are to be seen on the Menard Country Club golf course.

These ruins of a replica of the San Sabá presidio are situated on the grounds of the Menard Country Club.

Ben Milam Led the Storming of Bexar

Benjamin Rush Milam, born in Frankfort, Kentucky, October 20, 1788, fought in the War of 1812, and was on his way to South America when the ship's captain and most of the crew died of yellow fever and the inexperienced passengers had to man the vessel. He traded with the Comanche in Texas in 1818 and was involved in the filibustering efforts of Dr. James Long and Jose Trespalacios. Milam was imprisoned by the Spaniards at Saltillo. He was six feet tall and weighed 200 pounds. Lamar wrote of him, "Milam, though at that time a very young man, almost destitute in education, was nevertheless remarkable for his good sense, sound discretion and dignified sobriety...."

Milam, a Catholic and a Mason, became a Mexican citizen in 1824 and devoted the next few years to developing empresario grants. In late 1834 he went to Monclova, the capital of Coahuila y Texas, to obtain titles for himself and his North Texas neighbors and got involved in a controversy growing out of Santa Anna's setting aside the Mexican constitution. He was imprisoned but escaped; on his return in October, 1835, he found the Texians at war against Santa Anna.

Milam participated in George Collinsworth's capture of Goliad and was with Stephen F. Austin's army as it laid siege to San Antonio. The Texians prevailed in a few small engagements, but no effort was made to invade the town, which was held by Santa Anna's brother-in-law, General Martín Perfecto de Cós. In late November Austin was commissioned to seek assistance in the United States, and on December 4 General Edward Burleson, Austin's successor, ordered a retreat to winter quarters at Gonzales or Goliad to begin the next day. Because of the lack of action only about 500 men still remained—once there had been twice that number. Many of the Texians feared that the army would simply dissolve if a withdrawal were made, and they were certain Cós would take advantage of their absence. Then a Mexican deserter confirmed Samuel Maverick's earlier report that the defenses were weak and San Antonio could be taken easily. Colonel Ben Milam urged, without success, that Burleson order an attack. Then, at the suggestion of Colonel Frank Johnson, Milam stepped before the crowd outside Burleson's tent and shouted, "Who will go into Bexar with old Ben Milam?"

Three hundred and one volunteers responded. They assembled at the Old Mill, 800 to 1,000 yards north of town, to storm San Antonio the next morning. Milam would lead the first division "by the first street running north from the public square," Acequia, and occupy the De la Garza house, which was "within musket range of the square." Johnson would go by way of the river down Soledad Street and seize the Juan Veramendi house. In the meantime Colonel James C. Neill, with one cannon, was to cross the river and open fire on the Alamo so that the advance of Milam and Johnson would not be noticed.

The Mexican defenders were divided into two forces, one holding the town and the other the Alamo. Cós, headquartered in the Hall of Justice on Constitution Plaza, had been busy preparing defensive positions. The Alamo was on high

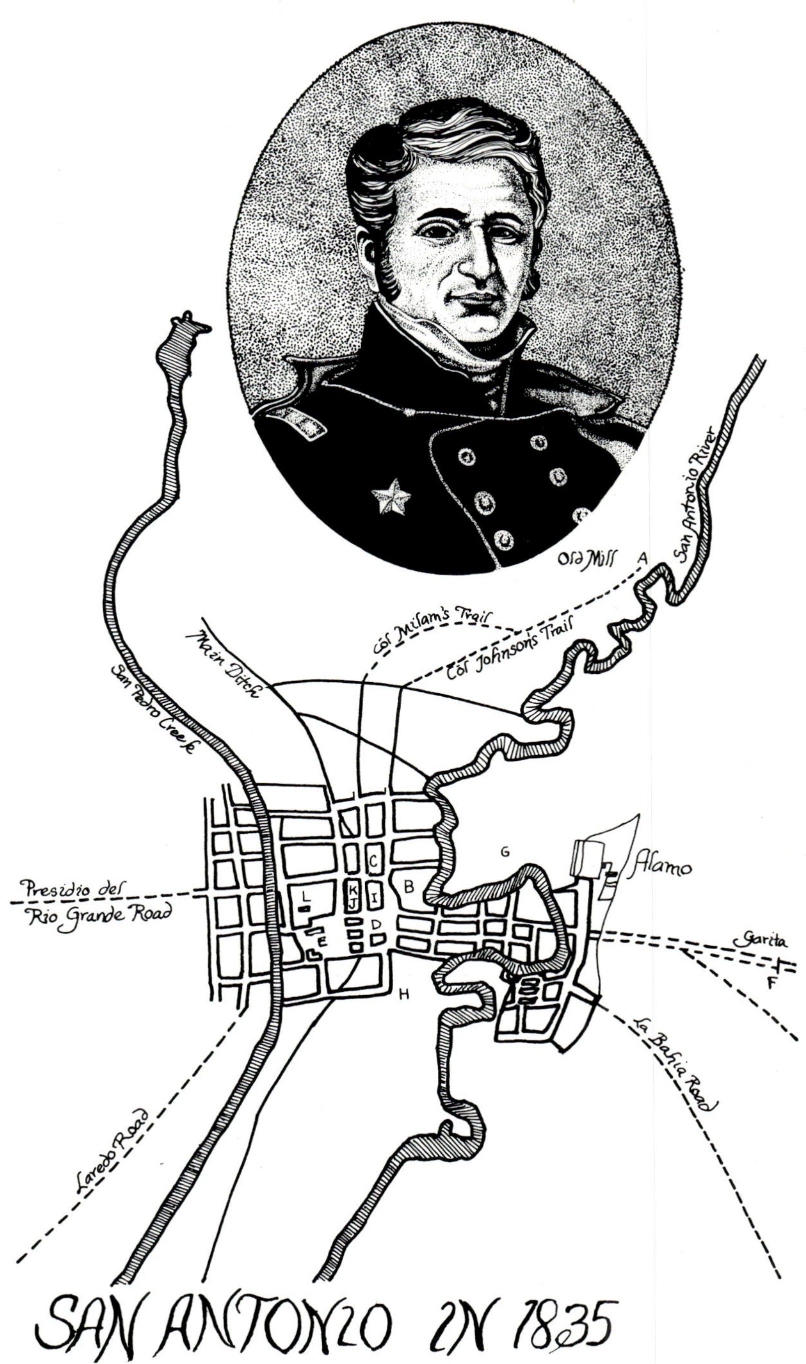

SAN ANTONIO IN 1835

A. Old Mill
B. Veramendi's House
C. Garza's House
D. Main Square, or Plaza de la Constiucion
E. Military Plaza
F. Powder-House, or Garita

G. Redoubt
H. Quinta
I. Priest's House
J. Antonio Navarro's House
K. Zambrano Row
L. Mexican Redoubt

ground, and the artillery placed in the top of its church, combined with the cannon high in the tower of the downtown church, commanded the entire area. Johnson described the defenses of Military and Constitution plazas—on either side of the church—in this fashion:

> ...a breastwork, and one gun was thrown up at the northeast angle of Constitutional Plaza, also a breastwork and gun at the entrance of the street from the Alamo, in Constitutional Plaza. At the southeast angle of the same plaza was another work and one gun. At the southwest angle of Military Plaza was another breastwork and at the northwest angle was erected a breastwork with one gun, and a furnace for heating shot. About midway of this plaza, north boundary, was a redoubt with three guns.

The invasion began from the Old Mill, some 800 yards north of the Alamo, just before dawn on December 5. While Neill was shelling the Alamo the Texians moved out. Hendrick Arnold, a black, guided the first division while his father-in-law, Deaf Smith, and John W. Smith took the second. The first division had farther to travel than the second and entered the town a few minutes later. With little difficulty the Veramendi and De la Garza houses were occupied; their thick walls would withstand light artillery fire. Then the Mexicans began firing from the Alamo and from Constitution Plaza, one block south of Johnson, who reported, "The fire of the enemy was so heavy that we could do but little more than strengthen our outer walls, secure the doors and windows with timber and sand-bags, cut loop-holes in the walls of the building, and use our rifles whenever a Mexican showed himself."

The heavy fire continued all day; the Texian casualties were one dead and about ten wounded. That night they began digging a trench to connect the two divisions. In the meantime Burleson held his force at the Old Mill to block attempts to reenforce Cós and, if necessary, to aid Milam and Johnson. The next day the second division advanced somewhat and the Texians were able to begin using a cannon from their new positions; their casualties were five wounded.

On the third day, December 7, Ben Milam was killed. Colonel Johnson wrote:

> ...at half past three o'clock, as our gallant commander, Colonel Milam, had entered the yard of the house occupied by the second division, he received a rifle shot in the head, which caused his instant death....When killed, the Masonic fraternity, then present, took charge of his body, and, with a proper detail of troops, he was buried in the yard—east side—of the Veramendi house, with military honors. His remains were subsequently disinterred and deposited in the old burying ground west of the town....

Creed Taylor, an eyewitness, stated:

> Milam carried a small field glass...whilst standing in the front yard of the building Milam was viewing the Mexicans' stronghold on the Plaza. At this moment a shot rang out and Milam fell, the shot piercing his head....One of those present in the yard called attention to the fact that at the report of the shot he saw a white puff of smoke rising from the branches of a large cypress tree that stood on the margin of the river. At this announcement all eyes were turned in the direction of that tree, the outline of a man was seen, several rifle shots rang out, and the corpse of the daring sharpshooter crashed down through the branches....After the surrender Col. Sanchez told...that this sharpshooter, Felix De La Garza, was the best shot in the Mexican army, half-brother of Almonte, and that General Cós was deeply grieved over his death.

Johnson succeeded Milam in command of the assault, and that evening the Jóse Navarro house was captured. On the fourth day, December 8, the Zambrano Row of buildings was taken as the Texians advanced from room to room, using crowbars to make holes in the walls through which they fired their rifles.

Before dawn on the fifth day the priest's house, just north of Constitution Plaza, was captured. A soldier wrote:

> The Priest informed us as soon as we got into the house that Ugartechea had just arrived in town with 1000 men and that he had no doubt but we would be all killed but we proceeded to dig up the dirt from the floor with our Bowie knives to help barricade the doors and windows. We also took the beds and trunk that were in the house to aid but as fast as we could put them up against the doors and windows they were shot out by the Cannon of the Enemy, several Balls came through and fell in the floor by us....

About daylight the Mexicans ceased firing and began a retreat. Under a white flag Cós informed the Texians that he wished to surrender. Cós had sustained heavy desertions; his supplies were badly depleted by the weeks of siege and the fighting, and the arrival of Ugartechea, with another 600 men who had to be fed, rendered the situation impossible.

On December 10, 1835, a capitulation was signed by Cós and Burleson providing for the surrender of about 1,400 Mexican soldiers and their withdrawal beyond the Río Grande on a parole whose terms bound Cós and his officers not "in any way to oppose the re-establishment of the Federal Constitution of 1824."

The scout Deaf Smith wrote a poem to Ben Milam's memory, which closes with, "As bright as thy example, so bright shall be thy fame, And generations yet unborn shall honor Milam's name."

John J. Linn authored a resolution providing for erection of a monument to Milam at San Antonio. It was adopted by the General Council 19 days after Milam's death, and Governor Henry Smith and Gail Borden were appointed to a committee charged with carrying out that resolution. John Henry Brown complained later, "Mr. Linn died in Victoria....Fifty-six years, less two months and two days, had passed since the adoption of his resolution and still there is no monument to Milam....Every man on that committee and every member of that council is dead, and still there is no monument to Milam! Will it forever be thus? God forbid!"

Statehood Was Proclaimed at Comanche Peak

From the earliest times men had considered the conspicuous 1229-foot Comanche Peak a special place. The Comanche used it as a rendezvous for members of war parties separated in battle. It was useful as a base camp where women and children might be left while the braves raided farther south, and the mesa was a splendid stage for victory dances.

Vance Maloney, who devoted much study to Comanche Peak, says early maps refer to it as "Lomo Alto" or simply "Peak" and that the Comanche called it "QUE-TAH-TO-YAH"—meaning "Rocky Butte"—a more appropriate name, since it is not a peak at all. Because of the misnomer, Cherokee agent Pierce M. Butler—a former South Carolina governor—and M.G. Lewis had a difficult time locating Comanche Peak in 1846. They were to assemble the Comanche for purposes of recovering captive white children and negotiating a peace treaty. From Coffee's place on Red River invitations were sent to the tribes for a Comanche Peak council. After failing to find a peak the commissioners split into four search parties; when, three weeks later, it was located, Cherokee delegate Elijah Hicks wrote, "Three men returned from Comanche Peak...It has been found at last but destitute of the enchantment. Low! It is a bushy hill!"

Members of the Five Civilized Tribes had come along to assist the commissioners. The Cherokee delegation included Sequoyah's son, Teesay Guess, and J.L. Washburn, editor of the Arkansas *Intelligencer*. The Seminole chief, Wild Cat, entertained Hicks with "remarks on the fine promises of Govt. officers in Florida to the Seminoleys. The (sic) had assured them that in the west, they would find amongst a numerous herds of Buffalows," but Wild Cat, after journeying 1500 miles, had just seen his first buffalo. Commissioner Lewis, traveling by wagon, had brought his wife, the only woman with 47 men, one of whom noted, "She is quite an Amazon...Wears a belt and dagger—shoots a rifle expertly—rides well on horseback and takes notes—rather handsome, medium size, English by birth—married four years—no children." Holland Coffee, proprietor of the Red River trading post, and his hunters provided meat for the group. Interpreters included the Delaware Jim Shaw and Cherokee Jesse Chisholm, whose name the great cattle highway to Kansas would later bear.

While efforts to bring in the Comanche continued, meetings were held with the Tonkawa, Lipan, and others. On March 5 the commissioners met with Buffalo Hump and asked him to persuade other Comanche chiefs to parley. Creek chief Chilly McIntosh explained the advantages of a great council, and Cherokee William Coodey announced that Texas had become part of the United States and henceforth the president would deal with the Indians. From the Comanche Peak meetings came the May 15, 1846, council held near Waco when about 122 Keechi, Tonkawa, Waco, Wichita, Comanche and others acknowledged American protection and promised to release white and negro prisoners.

John F. Torrey, a proprietor of the Torrey trading houses, took title to Comanche Peak in 1847 but did not live there for almost a quarter of a century.

The Comanche Peak has always been an important landmark in the vicinity of Hood County.

The Alabama and Coushatta Settled in Texas

In 1541 the De Soto expedition encountered the Alabama Indians in Northern Mississippi—the chronicler called them "Alibamo"—and by 1700 they were living on the Alabama River in the present state of Alabama. The Coushatta, or Koosati, were found on the Tennessee River in De Soto's time, but before 1684 they settled near the Alabama, west of the confluence of the Coosa and Tallapoosa Rivers; they spoke a Muskhogean language similar to that of their kinsmen, the Alabama. Both tribes belonged to the Creek confederacy, so named by the English because of their land's many streams. The Coushatta village was a white, or peace, town; the Alabama lived in a red, or war, town. The designation of the fifty or so Creek villages as "white" or "red" was of much early significance but finally controlled only the scheduling of ball games.

The Alabama and Coushatta were friends of the French, who taught that the English intended to exterminate them. When the British became owners of their country in 1763, many Alabama and Coushatta moved away to Texas' Red and Sabine rivers, where the country resembled that they had always known and the game was similar to that of Alabama. More importantly, the new country was apparently beyond the reach of Europeans; those who claimed to own it lived far away in Mexico.

The Louisiana Purchase caused another migration from Alabama, for the distrust of the English carried over to the Americans, who spoke the same language. About 1809 the Alabama and Coushatta moved further west to the Neches River in Spanish Texas, where they built two villages 40 miles apart. Their legends of origin teach that the Alabama and Coushatta have always been related. At the creation they emerged from the earth on opposite sides of the roots of a tree, and they have remained neighbors throughout history. A Mexican census of Indians in 1831 reflected 600 Alabama in three villages on the Neches and 400 Coushatta on the Trinity. They lived in log houses, raised corn, kept orchards, and sold furs to traders at Nacogdoches. The men did the farm work, except when away on hunting trips, and treated their women better than most Indians.

In 1836 most of the Alabama and Coushatta still in the old country moved to the Indian Territory with the rest of the Creek; members of both tribes live in Oklahoma today. Sam Houston, always the friend of the Indian, advised the Alabama to remain neutral during the Texas revolution. Their neutrality may have been the reason they moved to Louisiana until the Texian victory at San Jacinto. The Coushatta did not leave but assisted the Texians who fled before the Mexican armies in the Runaway Scrape. Even President M.B. Lamar, whose Indian policy was always negative, protected the Alabama and Coushatta, promising "that they shall not be molested or interrupted in the peaceful enjoyment of their possessions so long as they continue the same amiable relationships toward the Government which they have hitherto preserved."

During the decade of the Republic there was an attempt to set aside land for these Indians, but when annexation came the two tribes still were without titles to the tracts they occupied. Since the Alabama and Coushatta wanted to remain in East Texas and feared removal to the Indian Territory or to the proposed Texas reservation

Members of the Alabama and Coushatta invite tourists to their reservation near Livingston, Polk County.

for all tribes on the upper Brazos, in 1854 Sam Houston and some Polk County citizens persuaded the state to buy for the Alabama 1280 acres—at $2 an acre—about 17 miles from Livingston. Title vested in the entire tribe and the land could not be sold. About 330 Alabama settled there. The legislature voted to buy 640 acres adjoining the Alabama tract for the Coushatta, in 1855, but the transaction was never completed, so the Coushatta, numbering only about 80 by then, lived wherever they could, some on Alabama land. The Civil War interrupted efforts to obtain more land for both tribes. Both Alabama and Coushatta braves were in state and Confederate service.

Presbyterian missionaries began working among the Alabama while John Scott was their chief; he died in 1913, after having led the Alabama 40 of his 107 years. In 1881 the Reverend and Mrs. L.W. Currie organized a church and erected a building, and in 1900 Dr. and Mrs. C.W. Chambers began 37 years of preaching, teaching and doctoring (although neither was a physician). They had to live off the reservation because the Alabama followed Sam Houston's advice against permitting white persons to occupy their land. The missionaries had only the most meager financial support from their churches, and they were resented by local residents who had been in the practice of cheating the Indians.

The Indians did not entirely give up their old religions. The Alabama worshipped Abba Mingo, the chief of the sky, and the Coushatta's main deity was Emila He Mikoo, the one "who never dies." The sacrifice and devotion of Dr. and Mrs. Chambers were such that when their house burned the Alabama invited them to build a new one on the council grounds beside the school and church, but the missionaries declined, reminding the Indians of Houston's injunction.

In 1928 the United States paid $29,000 for 3,071 acres of land adjoining the original tract, which it holds in trust for the Alabama. The state and federal governments appropriated funds for the reservation in subsequent years. It was difficult to persuade the Indians to use the Livingston physician whose services Texas provided, and the people avoided the hospital because the whites had built it so near the burial grounds that spirits might move inside from the graves during the night. Frame houses built by the state often were not used. McConico Battise said:

> You see my old log house... I built that house in 1904. I cut every log and every shingle by hand. I bought nothing but the nails. You can see how solid it is now. But that government house, only 10 years old, is getting bad now....The new houses aren't good for the Indians. They are too tight. In the old days, too, when a person with a contagious disease died his family burned his house down, moved away and built a new one. Now the sickness stays on and collects in the new houses because it costs too much to build another one with mill lumber.

With the acceptance of government money came concessions such as allowing white teachers and nurses to live on the reservation. But the Indians followed Houston's advice in forbidding marriage to outsiders, although marriage to whites had occurred in earlier times.

W.E.S. Dickerson wrote that in 1940 there were 56 households on the reservation, and the six households outside the boundary were all Coushatta. One desiring to build a house on the reservation simply chose an unoccupied piece of land, got the chief's permission, and built there. While land and timber were still owned by the whole tribe, the mother owned the house and the children were members of her clan. Clan membership was formerly of great importance, for, among other things, it determined the suitability of a marriage partner. One could not marry within his own clan. Of the eleven clans represented on the reservation in 1940, two were destined for extinction, since the Wolf clan had only two members and the Alligators only one: all three were men, and since children were of the mother's clan there was no way these might be replaced.

Marriage to an Alabama is the only way the Coushatta are privileged to reside on the reservation, so most live outside.

Dan Waggoner Founded a North Texas Empire

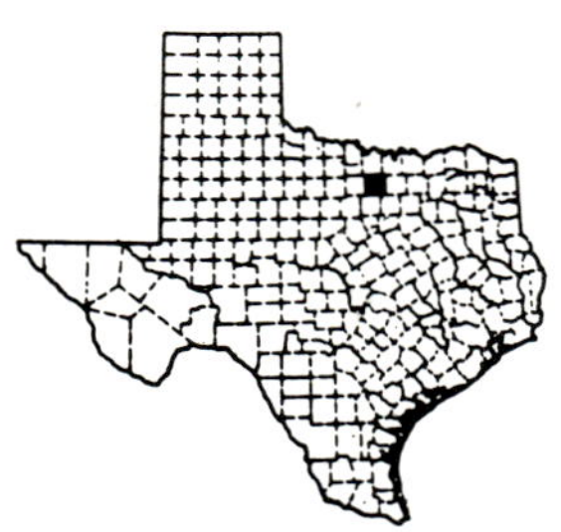

Dan Waggoner, born July 7, 1828, in Lincoln County, Tennessee, came with his parents to Hopkins County, Texas, in the forties. He had bought a herd consisting of an unspecified number of cattle—the bill of sale simply conveying all animals bearing a certain brand—which gave Waggoner ample reason to claim every maverick he found. In 1851 he took his wife, son and a slave boy to Wise County, where he ranched 15,000 acres some 18 miles west of Decatur, on the frontier, if not beyond it. Waggoner spent many days away from home chasing Indian war parties. Mrs. Waggoner and their son, William Thomas, regularly hid in the cornfield as Indians came to the place; for their protection Waggoner moved eastward to Denton Creek. After the death of his first wife, Nancy Moore, he married Electious Halsell's daughter, Scylly Ann, and they lived in a log dugout in Decatur.

Waggoner's son, William Thomas, who was born August 31, 1853, in Hopkins County and would develop the half-million-acre Waggoner Ranch, was doing a man's work at the age of fourteen. Texas cattle increased considerably during the Civil War, and about 1866 Dan Waggoner began grazing his herds in Clay County. About 1869, doing business as D. Waggoner and Son, the Waggoners trailed a herd to Kansas and sold it for $55,000, a fantastic sum in a country drained of capital. Moving further west they headquartered northwest of Wichita Falls for awhile and then moved to the China Creek place north of present Electra.

The Waggoners were using the three-D brand by 1881; it was a hard brand to alter, and cowboys said that reversing the D's made them more easily seen from the front. The Waggoners were buying huge tracts in Wilbarger, Foard, and other counties; when asked if he intended to own all the land in North Texas, Dan Waggoner answered, "No, only what adjoins me." They soon owned a thirty-mile stretch along Red River. In a single month W.T. bought 25,000 acres. About 1883 they began leasing about half a million acres of grassland across Red River in the Indian Territory. They had stopped adding to their holdings, but when it appeared that the United States was considering the termination of the practice of Indians leasing their land the Waggoners resumed buying. In 1900 the lessees were given a year within which to vacate their Indian holdings.

The removal order caused some serious problems; several thousand head would have to be relocated, and the land adjoining the Waggoners in Texas had been bought by other ranchers and a few farmers. Within a decade, beginning about 1896, the Waggoners accumulated some 500,000 acres in Wilbarger, Baylor, Foard, Knox, Archer, and Wichita Counties. Sachueista, 17 miles south of Vernon, became the headquarters. The ranch land along the Red River was sold for farming as cheaper pastures were purchased farther west.

In 1877 W.T. Waggoner married Ella Halsell, the younger sister of his father's second wife. Two of their five children, Daniel and Willie Tom, died young; the others were Paul, Guy, and Electra. Tom Waggoner worked alongside his cowhands, as did most of the great cattlemen. About 1885 the Waggoners began to upgrade their herds

Dan Waggoner built his mansion on a hill above Decatur.

through the use of Hereford and Shorthorn bulls. Their three and four-year-old steers weighed between 1,000 and 1,200 pounds. Because they performed best, the herds came to consist mainly of Herefords.

W.T. Waggoner had always idolized his father. Both lived in the $50,000 stone mansion Dan Waggoner built on a hill above Decatur. The elder Waggoner's death, in Colorado Springs, in September, 1904, was a heavy blow to the son. In addition it came at that particularly bad time when they were forced to buy new Texas land to graze the cattle they were having to move out of the Comanche big pasture in the Indian country.

Stories about the Waggoners abound in North Texas; most concern Dan's wealth and frugality. My grandmother tells of Dan always tamping out his cigar stub and leaving it on top of a fencepost—to be reclaimed and relighted later—as he entered her step-mother's Decatur boarding house to patronize the dining room. He had a reputation for feeding his cowhands on strays from other ranchers' herds; once, while on a trail drive, another cowman invited him to supper, promising something Dan Waggoner had never tasted before. After the meal Waggoner complimented the cook but said he had noticed nothing new. His host then stated Waggoner had just helped consume a three-D beef, a taste sensation Waggoner had never yet experienced. And once W.T. Waggoner was on an Oklahoma train when it was boarded by robbers, who began taking the passengers' valuables. A gunman recognized Waggoner and was furious when he found that the cattleman had nothing of value on him. He stormed, "Next time you ride a train I rob you damn well better have more than two or three dollars on you."

Although eventually he would become an oil millionaire, W.T. Waggoner was not pleased at discovering, in 1903, that there was petroleum under his land; he had contracted for a water well at what is now the intersection of Bryan and Waggoner streets in the city of Electra. When the drillers struck oil, they were ordered to desist and try for water at another location. The result was the same and Waggoner, trying to provide water for his stock, complained, "Oil, nothing but oil. It's water I want." The wells were abandoned, and ranchers used the oil which rose to the surface of the ground as cattle dip. Later, after the Electra boom began, in 1911, W.T. Waggoner opened his land to oil prospecting, but he never ceased complaining about the drilling crews, charging, "They leave my gates open." He built a refinery—that produced 7.5 million gallons of 3D gasoline in 1928—hundreds of filling stations, and some tall buildings in Fort Worth.

On Christmas Day, 1909, W.T. Waggoner gave each of his children, Electra—Mrs. A.B. Wharton—Guy, and Paul about 85,000 acres, 1,000 horses, 10,000 cattle, and everything else necessary in the operation of a ranch. These gifts, worth some $2 million apiece, left Waggoner with about 255,000 acres; he told the *Star-Telegram*, "I have had to work hard for every cent I have. I want my children to have an easier lot in life. If they are careful they can become independently wealthy." After thirteen years the three ranches were merged under a trust agreement and managed by W.T. Waggoner as trustee.

Because of his love of horses it was natural that W.T. Waggoner be interested in racing. He had a private race track where he delighted in beating Burk Burnett and other friends. He was proud of his race horses and was always trying to improve his stock. In 1931 he built and equipped Arlington Downs, a two-million-dollar facility and one of the best in the country; the next step was for Texas

Dan Waggoner began ranching in frontier Wise County 125 years ago.

to legalize race-track betting, which had been outlawed since 1909. Waggoner succeeded in May, 1933, just as he suffered a serious paralytic stroke. Representatives of the nation's great stables came to Arlington Downs, and Waggoner's 3D string raced under their red, white, and blue silks. The stroke made it impossible for Waggoner to see the races, but his driver brought him to the track to hear the crowd and to pet his horses as they were led to his car. He died December 11, 1934, in Fort Worth.

In June, 1937, a special session of the legislature repealed the pari-mutuel betting law, and the Waggoners closed Arlington Downs. Much later the property was sold to the Great Southwest Corporation; SIX FLAGS OVER TEXAS and the Great Southwest Industrial District were built there.

W. T. Waggoner became his father's partner in the cattle business when he was only a boy.
Among his friends was humorist Will Rogers.

Richard King Began Ranching on Santa Gertrudis Creek

Richard King was born in New York City on July 10, 1824, to poor Irish immigrants who apprenticed him to a jeweler at the age of nine; two years later he stowed away on the *Desdemona*, a sailing ship whose captain permitted him to remain as cabin boy. In time King became a riverboatman and pilot. He was working in Florida in 1843 when he met Mifflin Kenedy, the Quaker captain of the steamboat *Champion.* Their friendship endured throughout their lives. Soon after the Mexican War broke out Kenedy began steamboating on the Río Grande, captaining Army vessels supplying troops in Mexico. He wrote Richard King about the opportunities and suggested that King come to work for him. Richard King reached Texas in 1847.

After the close of the war King and Kenedy remained in the Lower Río Grande Valley, where they operated steamboats under the name of M. Kenedy & Co. In his years on the river King had wondered many times about the vast empty country to the north, so in 1852—when Henry Kinney held his Lone Star Fair at the village of Corpus Christi—King took that opportunity to journey through that land. Kinney had founded the town, and he advertised the fair as far away as Europe, hoping to build a population at the place he called "The Italy of America." Riding horseback the 165 miles from Brownsville to Corpus Christi, King decided that country would be a fine place for cattle. In the next year he bought 15,500 acres on Santa Gertrudis Creek. It was the beginning of the King Ranch, which would reach half a million acres in his lifetime.

In 1854 King married Henrietta Chamberlain, the daughter of Brownsville's Presbyterian minister, and took her to the ranch. Tom Lea, in his superb books on the ranch, quoted Mrs. King—recalling those days, after the passage of half a century—in the following fashion:

> When I came as a bride in 1854, the little ranch home then—a mere jacal as Mexicans would call it—was our abode for many months until our main ranch dwelling was completed....I remember that my pantry was so small my large platters were fastened to the walls outside.

Shortly before secession King and Kenedy formed a ranching partnership under the name of R. King & Co. Their steamboat business flourished during the Civil War as they helped feed Confederate troops and shipped cotton into Mexico to trade for badly needed arms and ammunition. After the war King and Kenedy, aware of how extensive their interests had become, feared the consequences to their partnership operations resulting from the death of one of them. They began dividing their land and the stock which ranged the unfenced country from the Nueces to the Río Grande. So great had their holdings become that more than 100 vaqueros spent a year locating and dividing the livestock.

From the beginning Captain King had had lawyers buying land to expand the ranch. The grants in the area were quite old, the land having been received by

Richard King, a steamboat captain, made the wilderness between the Nueces and the Río Grande inhabitable.

individuals who never tried to live there or who, attempting to occupy it, were driven away by drouth, Indians, and badmen. There was no market for the land. As time passed the grantees died, and their descendants were not interested in the property; even so deeds had to be purchased from each of the numerous heirs. Sometimes the same piece of land would be bought and paid for a dozen times and the process would take several years. Robert J. Kleberg, of Corpus Christi, and James B. Wells, of Brownsville, were the attorneys King used in acquiring the spread he called the Rancho Santa Gertrudis or King's Rancho. Counties bear the names of both attorneys: Kingsville is the seat of Kleberg County, and Alice—for the captain's daughter, Alice Gertrudis King—is the capital of Jim Wells County.

The steamboat business was sold by King and Kenedy during the seventies, while they were sending thousands of cattle from their adjoining ranches up the trail to Kansas. Life between the Río Grande and the Nueces was still dangerous because of raiding bandits from below the border. The Kings traveled to and from the ranch accompanied by armed guards, and when Captain King went to Brownsville alone he used the horses he maintained in camps about 20 miles apart, relying for protection upon the speed of his fresh mounts. While still trailing their cattle to the Kansas markets, King and Kenedy were prime movers in the construction of the Texas-Mexican Railway, which connected Corpus Christi and Laredo, in 1881.

Robert E. Lee King, the captain's younger son, died in St. Louis in 1893. Just before the marriage of the other son, Richard King, II, Captain King gave him the 40,000-acre Rancho Puerta de Agua Dulce. Two of his daughters lived in St. Louis; Henrietta was married to E. B. Atwood, and Ella King was Mrs. Louis Walton. The youngest daughter, Alice Gertrudis King, remained at the 600,000-acre ranch; she would marry Robert Kleberg, who became Mrs. King's ranch manager after the captain's death.

Not long after Richard King, III, was born in late 1884, Captain King journeyed to San Antonio for treatment of severe stomach pains he had endured for years. He took rooms at the Menger Hotel, where Dr. Ferdinand Herff diagnosed his illness as cancer and cared for him. Captain King's children and friends—including Mifflin Kenedy—came to see him once more, and he died at the Menger on April 14, 1885.

By his industry and courage Captain King brought civilization to the big, empty, hazardous country between the Nueces and the Río Grande.

Bob Kleberg, a grandson of Captain Richard King, during his years as manager of the King Ranch worked cattle alongside his cowhands.

The Klebergs Developed the King Ranch

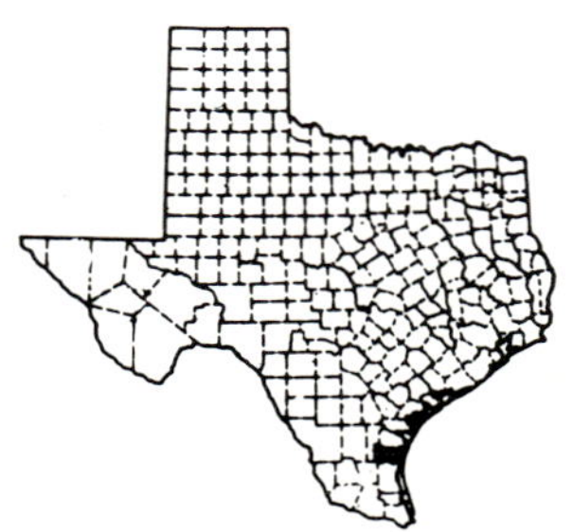

Robert Justus Kleberg was born in 1803 in Westphalia, Germany and graduated from the University of Goettingen with the Juris Doctor degree. He came to Texas in late 1834 and fought at San Jacinto as a member of Mosely Baker's company. He was the De Witt County Judge, and Kleberg County was named for him. His sons became lawyers: Marcellus was a Galveston legislator, Rudolph served in Congress, and Robert was practicing in Corpus Christi when he began representing Captain King.

Robert Justus Kleberg, II, born in 1853, attended Concrete College and became the county clerk at Cuero. His law degree was conferred by the University of Virginia in 1880, and Richard King hired him the following year. After the captain's death Mrs. King made Kleberg the manager of King's Rancho, and in 1886 he married Alice Gertrudis King.

Richard King's estate was appraised at just over a million dollars, but the captain was also heavily in debt. Kleberg began building on the foundation laid by King, impeded by economic conditions and drouth. One large chore involved ridding the ranch of hordes of worthless mustangs; 4,000 of the wild horses were captured in one haul, but many years of effort were required to get all of them. Kleberg increased the ranch to almost 1.2 million acres and imported Herefords and Durham Shorthorns to upgrade the herds. Captain King had brought in blooded cattle, too, with little success. Most died of Texas fever, the same malady that had provoked other states into passing laws against trail herds from Texas; no one knew just why, but the presence of healthy South Texas cattle caused the domestic stock to die in places such as Missouri and Kansas. As Kleberg watched bulls raised in colder climates sicken and die on the King Ranch he began to suspect that ticks carried the fever to which South Texas cattle had developed an immunity, scientists of the Department of Agriculture confirmed this suspicion in experiments conducted at the King Ranch in 1893. Kleberg devised methods for dealing with the fever, and his work in this field was probably his main contribution to the cattle industry and the state.

Perhaps Robert Kleberg's greatest contribution to the ranch was the development of a surface water supply in response to the rancher's quandry that Captain King had cast in terms of: "Where I have grass, I have no water. And where I have water, I have no grass....Things are getting in a hell of a fix fast." The 150-mile strip between the Nueces and Río Grande had no streams which flowed year round and only 5% of the pastures could be grazed because of lack of drinking water. Kleberg built dams to impound surface water and drilled wells. With plenty of artesian water available he experimented with various crops, including cotton, cabbage, onions, and grain feed. The fruit trees Kleberg imported and the experts he hired to handle them demonstrated that oranges and grapefruit would thrive in South Texas.

With proof that farming was possible and with the completion, in 1904, of

Bob Kleberg cuts a yearling out of a King Ranch herd of Santa Gertrudis cattle.

the St. Louis, Brownsville and Mexico Railway—Robert J. Kleberg, Vice President, and John G. Kenedy, Secretary—the next step in development of the area was the founding of towns. Where the new railroad's tracks crossed those of the Tex-Mex in Robert Driscoll's pasture, Robstown was founded. Three miles east of King Ranch headquarters the Kleberg Town and Improvement Company had laid out Kingsville before the new railroad's arrival; Mrs. King's lumber yard and the Kleberg Bank were the town's first permanent businesses. Because of the Presbyterian beliefs of Mrs. King, Kingsville had no Sunday rail service, and deed restrictions prohibited the sale of liquor there. Within two years the town had 1,000 residents.

Mrs. Henrietta King died in 1925; her will provided that trustees operate the ranch for ten years. Robert Kleberg died in 1932, and when the trusteeship ended, three years later, Alice King Kleberg conveyed her inheritance—some 458,000 acres—to the King Ranch, a corporation owned by her five children. By 1953, a hundred years after Captain King's original purchase, the King Ranch consisted of 940,000 acres and grazed about 80,000 head of cattle and 3,000 horses.

The older son of Robert and Alice Kleberg, Richard Mifflin—named for his grandfather and Mifflin Kenedy—served half a dozen terms in Congress, where the very young Lyndon Baines Johnson was his secretary. Both Richard Kleberg and his father were president of the Southwestern Cattle Raisers Association and his brother, Robert—the third Robert Justus Kleberg—was an honorary vice-president for more than a quarter of a century. Because of his father's long illness, Robert Kleberg, Jr., became the acting manager of the ranch during World War I; he continued to manage it until his death in October, 1974. Of the three daughters of Robert and Alice King Kleberg, Henrietta married John Larkin and, following his death, Tom Armstrong; Alice married Tom East; and Sarah married Henry Johnson, Jr., and, after his death, Dr. Joseph Shelton.

Nine hundred King Ranch employees work 860,000 South Texas acres now. In addition the ranch has extensive operations in Florida, Pennsylvania, Kentucky, Venezuela, Brazil, Argentina, Spain, Morocco and Australia.

Governor Buford Jester and Congressman Richard Mifflin Kleberg admire the King Ranch Triple Crown winner, Assault.

The Santa Gertrudis Was the First American Breed

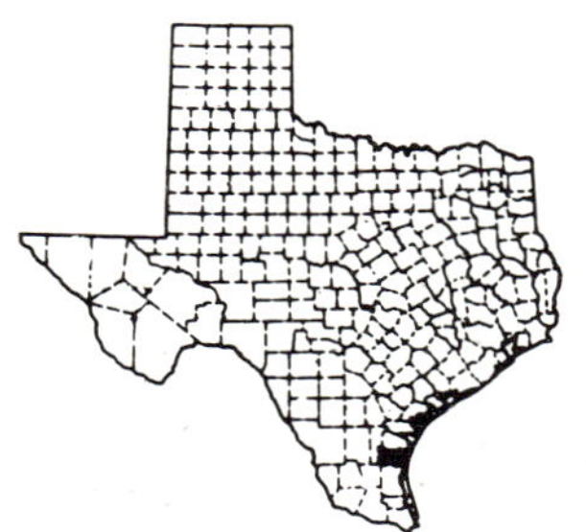

When Captain Richard King began ranching his stock consisted of Longhorns, hardy descendants of cattle the conquistadors had brought from Spain; during their three and a half centuries in this hemisphere they developed long legs, long bodies and formidable horns. Cowhands found them difficult to handle but they were ideal for trail driving; their horns guaranteed sufficient air space between animals to avoid the overheating which caused weight loss and, too often, death. But the tough Longhorns did not produce the choice grades of beef for which buyers paid top prices.

Captain King attempted, without much success, to upgrade his herds. Soon after the close of Reconstruction he bought 100 Durham bulls and was fencing his land for breeding control, but these efforts were premature; too many other tasks required attention, and until railroads reached the area and trail driving passed into disuse, King could not afford to own blooded animals which were unable to walk to Kansas.

Robert Kleberg began buying Durham Shorthorns and Herefords in 1886, and for years some 4,000 purebred Shorthorns and 2,500 Herefords were kept to provide bulls for improving range stock. The objective was to produce as much choice beef per acre as possible. He raised the overall quality of the King Ranch herds significantly, but some problems had become apparent. While infusion of the blood of these English breeds produced better beef animals, they lacked the resistance to heat, insects and diseases possessed by Longhorns. Furthermore, the new blooded stock was not as prolific as Texas cattle. Robert Kleberg, Jr., believed this lost hardiness and fertility could be recovered by the use of Brahman bulls. Brahman cattle, brought from India about the turn of the century, prospered despite heat and drought. They not only possessed the desired tough, Longhorn characteristics but they were much larger animals. In 1910 Tom O'Connor, of Victoria, had given Mrs. King a half-Brahman, half-Shorthorn bull, whose offspring were far superior to those of the Shorthorn bulls. Robert Kleberg, Jr., persuaded his father to let him implement a program using Brahman bulls and Shorthorn cows to produce a new beef type. The elder Kleberg was understandably reluctant; it had taken a third of a century to develop on the King Ranch the nation's largest herds of Herefords and Shorthorns, and experts warned against crossing purebred cattle. There was much to lose if the experiment failed.

The object was not merely to produce a crossbreed but an entirely new breed, something which had not been done in nearly two hundred years. Albert O. Rhoad described the endeavor as "putting together combinations of genes that heretofore had not existed and concentrating the desirable new combinations into a uniform breeding population." Instead of continuing to breed Brahmans to Shorthorns to get the kind of cattle he wanted, Robert Kleberg, Jr., intended to develop an animal which could reproduce his characteristics in his offspring.

In 1918 the ranch bought from A.P. Borden fifty-two bulls, each three-fourths to seven-eighths Brahman. These three-year-old bulls were divided among eight herds of

The King Ranch owned huge herds of purebred Shorthorns and Herefords, but these animals were not sufficiently hardy for the climate of South Texas. Robert Kleberg, Jr., began trying to develop a tougher beef animal. Monkey, born in 1920, became the sire of this first American breed, the Santa Gertrudis; of Brahman and Shorthorn ancestry, they thrive on grass.

purebred Shorthorn cows. One of the Brahmans, Vinotero, was mated with a Shorthorn cow who was one-sixteenth Brahman by virtue of descent from the O'Connor bull; the resulting bull calf, Monkey—born in 1920 and died in 1932—fit the specifications set by the Klebergs: Robert, Jr., his brother, Richard, and his cousin, Caesar. At age one Monkey weighed 1,100 pounds and had the desired conformation and red color, and he was able to transmit these characteristics to his offspring. Monkey is the sire of the Santa Gertrudis breed, the ancestor of the first strain of cattle developed in the United States and the first new breed in two centuries. His descendants improved the breed. The best producer of his 150 useful sons was Santa Gertrudis, but his best son was Tipo, and Tipo's best son was Coton. The Santa Gertrudis, three-eighths Brahman and five-eighths Shorthorn, was recognized as a new breed by the United States Bureau of Animal Husbandry in July, 1940.

Santa Gertrudis cattle have longer bodies than Brahmans and are not so wild. Under identical range conditions in South Texas a full-grown Santa Gertrudis will weigh 300 pounds more than a Hereford or Shorthorn. They withstand heat, drought, insects, and disease much better than the British breeds. They are also more accomplished rustlers than their competitors, meaning that they are more efficient converters of grass into beef, but probably their most important characteristic is the ability to gain weight rapidly on grass alone. King Ranch geneticist Albert O. Rhoad said:

> The creation of the Santa Gertrudis breed has a definite significance to the livestock industry: Ranchers in the Southwest and in many other unfavorable environments of the world confronted with problems of deterioration of their cattle because of difficult environments now have an improved beef breed of predominantly European origin adapted to harsh conditions....

By 1975 there were Santa Gertrudis in 47 states, Cuba, Mexico, Canada, the Philippines, and forty other countries.

The stable bears the brown and white racing colors of the King Ranch and displays the running snake brand.

Assault Won the Triple Crown of Racing

From the beginning Richard King bought fine horses to upgrade his stock, bringing some of them from Kentucky and paying up to $1,000 for a good stallion. The Klebergs were as interested in horse breeding as Captain King had been. Just prior to the turn of the century the King Ranch was selling thousands of horses each year. It was, in fact, one of the largest producers in the world because of the quality produced by the addition of thoroughbred blood to range stock.

In 1916 Robert Kleberg, Jr., not yet old enough to vote, saw a herd of horses he admired and got his cousin, Caesar, to buy a stud colt from that group. In this fashion, for $125, the sorrel horse was acquired; Old Sorrel became the sire of the King Ranch Quarter Horses. He was intelligent, agile, and strong. A.O. Rhoad stated: "When he was broken and tried for cattle work Old Sorrel proved to be outstandingly the best cow horse we had ever had on King Ranch. He was exceptional as to beauty, disposition, conformation, smoothness of action and fine handling qualities....we determined, if possible, to perpetuate the wonderful qualities of this stallion." When the American Quarter Horse Association issued the first registration number in its first stud book it was to Wimpy, the Grand Champion Stallion of the 1941 Fort Worth Fat Stock Show. Wimpy was the grandson of Old Sorrel.

It was the desire to continue improving their quarter horses that led the Klebergs into horse racing. While buying a mare in 1934, Robert Kleberg, Jr., happened to see Chicaro, a race horse who was well past his prime, and bought him. Chicaro, sired by Chicle, was descended from a line that had produced Twenty Grand, winner of the Kentucky Derby in record time. Much later, on a trip to Kentucky, Kleberg noticed Cornsilk, a mare with the best conformation he had ever seen. As he was attempting to buy her he learned that she was a daughter of Chicle; both Chicaro and Cornsilk were descended from Domino and Commando.

Two years after Bold Venture—of the Domino-Commando line—won the 1936 Kentucky Derby and the Preakness, Kleberg bought him, intending to blend this blood line with that of Fair Play through Man o' War. Before long, horses bearing the brown and white colors of the King Ranch were winning races. In 1943, failing to recognize his potential, Kleberg sold Stymie in a $1,500 claiming race; Stymie won $918,455 for his new owners.

Three years later Assault, Bold Venture's son out of Igual, won the Kentucky Derby, the Preakness, and the Belmont Stakes; in more than a century only eight others were able to win the Triple Crown. The Clubfoot Comet, as he was called after injuring his right front hoof on a surveyor's stake, weighed only 970 pounds and began his career looking like anything but a champion. He finished twelfth in his first race and fifth in the second. His first win was at Aqueduct on July 19, 1945, but he lost more races than he won that year. In 1946 he took the Experimental Free Handicap at Jamaica and the Wood Memorial, but the odds against him were eight to one at Churchill Downs when the Kentucky Derby was run. With Warren Mehrtens up, he won by eight lengths. In his career Assault earned $675,470; he

Assault—the son of 1936 Kentucky Derby and Preakness winner Bold Venture—won those two races as well as the Belmont Stakes in 1946. Only eight other horses have won the Triple Crown in more than a century.

was put out to pasture in 1950.

In the year of Assault's retirement, Middleground, another son of Bold Venture, won the Kentucky Derby and the Belmont Stakes but lost the Preakness. Middleground was retired that year because of injuries, but he had won $237,725.

Other King Ranch thoroughbreds included Rejected, who won $544,000, and the Belmont Stakes winner, High Gun. In 1954 the ranch was the leading owner of racing horses, with winnings of $837,615. The ranch held second place in 1946, 1947 and 1948, when it won some $1.7 million. Overall the operation has probably been profitable; between 1935 and 1953, $1,773,000 was paid for race horses, and purse winnings amounted to $4,009,991.12. Gallant Bloom won $220,514 through 1969 and was the nation's best three-year-old filly in 1970.

The sire of the King Ranch Quarter Horses was Old Sorrel. Acquired in 1916, he was considered the best cowhorse the ranch ever owned.

Mifflin Kenedy Was a Steamboat Captain

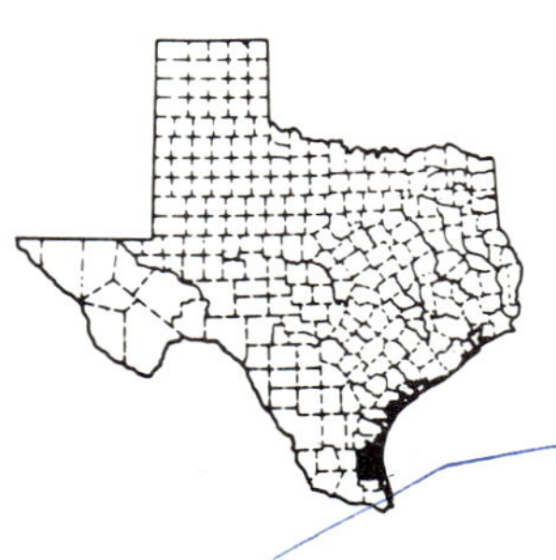

Mifflin Kenedy, born in Chester County, Pennsylvania in 1818, went to sea when he was 16 years old, sailing for Calcutta aboard the *Star*. He worked on Mississippi River steamboats, got his master's papers, and in 1843 was steamboating in Florida when he met Richard King. Early in the Mexican War Kenedy was in Pittsbugh having repairs made to his boat when he was hired by the Army to haul freight for Zachary Taylor's troops. From the Río Grande Kenedy sent word asking Richard King to come to Texas and serve as his pilot. After the war Kenedy promoted the new town of Roma, hoping to capture some of the business then going to Río Grande City, but Roma did not flourish. Kenedy imported goods into Mexico for awhile, then in 1850—with Richard King and Charles Stillman, of Brownsville—he formed M. Kenedy & Co. to haul freight on the Río Grande; M. Kenedy & Co. was a major factor in the local economy for almost a quarter of a century.

In 1852 Kenedy married Petra Vela de Vidal, the 26-year-old widow of a Mexican Army colonel and mother of five. Her family had come from Greece by way of Spain to Mexico, and her father was killed about 1832 by Indians who captured her three sisters. Two were later ransomed or escaped but the third sister was never again heard from, although an uncle spent many years searching for her.

Kenedy bought some ranch land about 60 miles above Brownsville, but steamboating required all of his time. After Juan Cortina raided him, Kenedy moved his remaining 1,600 head of cattle and his horses up to King's Rancho Santa Gertrudis, which he hoped was out of the reach of the border bandits. In 1860, with some other partners, Kenedy and King—each owning a 3/8ths interest—organized R. King and Co. to conduct their ranching business. While King ran the ranch Kenedy operated the boats; both ventures prospered. During the Civil War they freighted cotton into Mexico for funds needed by the Confederacy to carry on the struggle. After one partner moved away and another died, King and Kenedy dissolved the ranching partnership, fearing the problems which would arise if one of them should die; as it was, some 100 cowhands were kept busy for a year in collecting and dividing their livestock.

After the partnership dissolution Kenedy began fencing his Laureles Ranch; the 131,000 acres were situated on a peninsula, making it unnecessary to enclose all four sides; even so, 30 miles of Louisiana pine fence was required. His share of the partnership cattle was about 25,000 head.

In 1870 Kenedy was a founder of the Stock Raisers Association of Western Texas, an organization committed to protecting ranchers from the rustlers who took an estimated one-third of their livestock into Mexico annually. King alone lost 33,827 head of cattle in four years. Old ranger John Ford wrote:

> It must be remembered that the cattle thieves were almost innumerable. They came from considerable distances in Mexico to engage in stripping those who had conquered them. It was a labor of love with

Steamboat Captain Mifflin Kenedy built the 400,000-acre La Parra Ranch in Kenedy County.

the Mexicans. Officers of the Mexican Army engaged in the business of robbing those who claimed the protection of the United States....Beef was sold in Matamoras at very low prices.

King and Kenedy were the principal sponsors of the Texas—Mexican Railway, which ran from Corpus Christi to Laredo and was completed in 1881. Anticipating the coming of the railroads they had sold the steamboat company a few years earlier.

In 1882 Kenedy sold the Laureles Ranch to a syndicate of Scots for $1.1 million. Then he began acquiring land for a new ranch, the La Parra. He had been living at Corpus Christi for several years.

Mifflin Kenedy's son, James, the La Parra manager, died of typhoid in December, 1884, and his wife died in the following March just before he learned of Richard King's terminal illness. Captain Kenedy was an executor of the King estate, and the first child of Alice and Robert Kleberg was named Richard Mifflin for King and Kenedy.

Captain King's widow built a house next door to the aged Mifflin Kenedy's Corpus Christi home; his adopted daughter, Carmen, lived with him. Four of his six children were dead; Sarah and her husband, Dr. Arthur E. Spohn, lived in Corpus Christi, and John managed the 390,000-acre La Parra Ranch. Three of his step-daughters were Brownsville residents and the other lived at Laredo.

Kenedy was still expanding the ranch and he was a principal supporter of a new railroad, the San Antonio and Aransas Pass, which connected Corpus Christi and San Antonio. He outlasted Richard King by ten years and died of a heart attack March 14, 1895. Tom Lea wrote in his fine work, *The King Ranch:*

> The next afternoon a sorrowing procession wound its way to the cemetery. There Corpus Christi's most eminent pioneer was buried with full Masonic honors while the Catholic Church bells, which he had presented in memory of Petra Vela, tolled his passing....Mifflin Kenedy joined his old partner, beyond the remembered sound of steamboat whistles on the Río Grande, beyond the remembered sound of Longhorn herds milling in the dust of the Wild Horse Desert.

Kenedy County was carved out of Willacy County—which was only ten years old—in 1921. Sarita—honoring the captain's granddaughter—had been the seat of Willacy but now became the Kenedy County capital. Sarita had been laid out in 1905. John G. Kenedy had given much land for the construction of the railroad and was promised that he would have a townsite. After the main line, depot and other town improvements had been completed, a San Antonio man pointed out that the company had located everything on his land. As a result the general manager of the road, in February, 1905, got 300 teams from the King and Kenedy ranches, tore up the tracks, moved them a mile to the east and laid them again, and then moved the buildings to the present site of Sarita. This work was begun at 6 p.m. on Saturday and finished in time for the arrival of the passenger train on Monday morning. Sarita's population is about 200; the entire county had 678 residents in 1970.

Although originally it was thought that the land was good for nothing but ranching, in the first decade of this century the Kenedy Ranch was growing enough cotton to require a gin in Sarita. The ranch also pioneered in citrus fruit; in 1904 it won first prize at the St. Louis World's Fair for lemons grown there.

John G. Kenedy, Jr., the grandson of Captain Kenedy, succeeded his father as manager of La Parra Ranch.

El Paso Became the Metropolis of the Pass

El Paso is the newest of the communities at the Pass of the North; the oldest grew up around the Guadalupe mission which was founded in 1659 by Fray García de San Francisco y Zuñiga and called Paso del Norte and El Paso until 1882, when the Chihuahua legislature named it Juárez. The Mexican city was 168 years old—the same number of years separating the American Declaration of Independence and the last days of World War II—before settlement began on the site of El Paso. Juan Ponce de Leon, a wealthy Paso del Norte businessman, in 1827 and 1830, applied for patents to the tract he had been using across the Río Grande; downtown El Paso is situated there now. The hands who farmed it lived there in a few shacks, but Ponce remained in Mexico.

After independence was won the territory at the Pass was part of the Republic of Texas, but no effective effort was made to exercise sovereignty over it. During and after the Mexican War and the gold rush, Americans were surprised by the fertility of the Río Grande Valley, and a few chose to settle there. In the meantime a change in the river's course had moved the main channel south of the island occupied by Ysleta, Socorro, and San Elizario; by treaty between Mexico and the United States everything north and west of the river was part of Texas.

James Magoffin arrived in 1848 to found an adobe trading post, and the community which grew up around it was Magoffinsville. Benjamin Franklin Coons was operating a store and freighting business on the old Ponce de Leon ranch in the following year, and the settlement which resulted was named Franklin, for Coons. It was also called El Paso, causing confusion since the name was also applied to the corridor through the mountains and the older and better-known Paso del Norte.

At the formation of El Paso County, in 1850, El Paso's population was only about 200; the county seat, San Elizario, with 1,200, was the largest settlement in West Texas. The Texas side of the river remained relatively undeveloped; a person traveling from one place to another in El Paso County might cross the river into Mexico, use the better roads there, and then recross near his destination.

The 1860 census showed El Paso to have 428 citizens: 298 white males, 129 white females, and one black male. There were seven Anglo—American women; twenty-one El Pasoans were born in Europe and 144 in the United States. Individuals with Spanish names numbered 263. W.W. Mills, who arrived two years before, described El Paso as a small adobe hamlet surrounded by gardens, orchards, and vineyards irrigated from the river. A ferry at the foot of El Paso Street took pedestrians across the Río Grande in canoes and wagons in flat boats and, "there was not a railroad or a telegraph station within a thousand miles from us."

San Elizario fell into decline after the Salt War, but El Paso did not become the main settlement of the county until the arrival of the railroad in 1881.

El Paso was a dusty frontier village in 1881.

San Jacinto Plaza has been used as a public square since settlement began at El Paso.

Modern El Paso extends along the Río Grande, with Juárez, Mexico, and the mountains in the background.

A Fort Was Built at the Pass

The first American soldiers at the Pass of the North were with Lt. Zebulon Pike; in 1807 they were brought there as Spanish prisoners, enroute to Chihuahua. The next, a regiment of Missouri volunteers commanded by Colonel Alexander Doniphan, arrived during the Mexican War; General Kearny had ordered them to Chihuahua. Attacked by Mexican troops on Christmas Day, 1846, about 30 miles north of the Pass, Doniphan, without losing a man, repulsed the charge at a cost of about 100 Mexican casualties. Doniphan was greeted cordially by the residents of Paso del Norte, and his regiment remained there 42 days.

The Río Grande became an important international boundary after the close of the Mexican War. Men who were there as soldiers returned to create the town on the Texas side. Because the Treaty of Guadalupe Hidalgo, signed February 2, 1848, required that the United States protect Mexico from raids by American Indians, troops were sent to defend the frontier; later they would aid goldseekers bound for California. The first soldiers occupied quarters on the old Ponce de Leon rancho, which was then owned by Benjamin Franklin Coons, and did not stay long. By general order dated November 7, 1848, units of the 3rd Infantry Regiment were ordered to El Paso, and on the following September 14 Major Jefferson Van Horne and four companies of the regiment completed the 673-mile journey from San Antonio. They were quartered on a ranch owned by W.T. Smith; after a couple of years they were sent to New Mexico, making the settlement vulnerable to Apache attack. The fort was re-established in January, 1854, and adobe quarters were built on the Magoffin ranch about a mile from the first site. It was known as the Post of El Paso until March, when it was designated Fort Bliss. The post occupied that location until 1868.

While publications of the Fort Bliss museum state that the post was named for Lt. Col. William Wallace Smith Bliss—Zachary Taylor's son-in-law—and the *El Paso Herald—Post* of February 27, 1931, claimed that it bore the name of Brigadier General John Bliss, of Mexican war fame, General Robert Lee Howze was convinced that Lt. Col. John Bliss, a War of 1812 veteran, was the officer for whom the honor was intended.

El Paso had 200 people and was still known as Franklin when it became a Butterfield Stage stop in 1858. It was a Confederate town; only two votes were cast against secession. In March, 1861, when General Twiggs surrendered all army property in Texas, James Magoffin took charge of Fort Bliss and the officers and men withdrew to San Antonio. Just before Union troops under Colonel J.H. Carleton captured Fort Bliss in August, 1862, the Confederates destroyed the buildings. Residents sympathetic to the South moved to Paso del Norte, which had troubles of its own when Benito Juárez overthrew Maximilian's government. Paso del Norte was Juárez' capital in 1865. The fighting on both sides of the Río Grande depopulated Paso del Norte and El Paso. Neither recovered until the coming of the railroads.

Fort Bliss was rebuilt and reoccupied after the end of the war—Carleton had not garrisoned El Paso—but the river had ruined much of the land, so in March, 1868, the

A replica of the old Fort Bliss chapel houses exhibits explaining the origins of the post and El Paso. An imaginative gardner has given a hedge the shape of a horse.

post was moved to higher ground. This third site, at the Concordia ranch, was occupied until January, 1877, when the troops were moved to Fort Davis and Fort Bliss was abandoned. No soldiers were stationed at the Pass when the Salt War occurred, but that violent episode demonstrated the necessity of a permanent garrison. The units which were then sent there found Fort Bliss in ruins; they occupied rented quarters in downtown El Paso and drilled in San Jacinto Plaza until a 135-acre tract was purchased near Hart's Mill. This fourth location was occupied in 1880 by two companies of the 10th Infantry. After a railroad right-of-way was granted through the parade ground in 1887, another move was necessary. A thousand-acre tract was obtained in late 1893; this fifth, and present, site has been expanded several times.

Fort Bliss was always an infantry post until the 4th Cavalry moved there in 1912. Two years later Brigadier General John J. Pershing took command. Just before World War I, while Pershing was chasing Pancho Villa, about 60,000 national guardsmen were living in tents at Fort Bliss. It was expanded several times, so that by 1941 the post proper was 5,000 acres in addition to about 400,000 acres used for firing and testing ranges. It was the nation's largest cavalry post. The First Cavalry was organized there in 1921, with Major General Howze its first commanding officer. Fort Bliss became the antiaircraft artillery center in World War II and has since been given responsibility for guided missiles. It became the Army Air Defense Center in 1957 and now occupies more than a million acres.

Fort Bliss, the old cavalry post, is now the Army Air Defense Center and is responsible for development of guided missile systems.

Kit Carson Took an Army to Adobe Walls

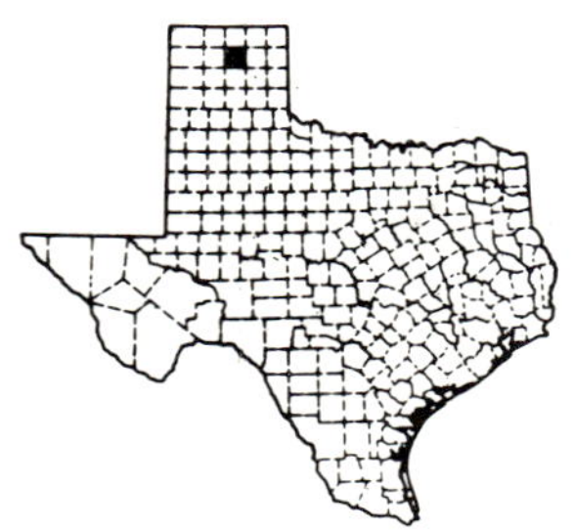

When the Civil War began, Christopher Carson was one of the best known men in the country. He had explored the west as the scout of John Frémont, the pathfinder, and Frémont's writings made Carson famous. Kit Carson was an Indian agent at Taos, New Mexico when he was commissioned as an Army lieutenant colonel in July, 1861, about the same time Frémont, the unsuccessful 1856 Republican presidential nominee, became the commanding general of the Department of the West.

In late 1864 Carson was ordered to make an expedition against the Kiowa and Comanche, who were wintering on the Canadian River in the Texas Panhandle. With 14 officers, 321 men, and 72 Ute and Apache scouts—and taking rations for 45 days—Carson left Fort Bascom, New Mexico, on November 6. Through bitter cold and snowstorms they followed the Canadian River. They were west of Adobe Walls, Hutchinson County, on November 24 when the scouts reported large numbers of hostile Indians in the vicinity.

On their eastern flank the plains tribes had been without restraints since 1861 when federal troops were withdrawn from Texas; the soldiers to the west were kept busy by the unruly Navaho. The Comanche and Kiowa had not only punished the Texas frontier—which was not the problem of the federals—but had raided Kansas and Colorado and disrupted travel over the Santa Fé trail. The Comanche and Kiowa had acquiesced in the trail's presence, but they complained that travelers did not keep to that road.

Early in the morning of the 25th, Carson attacked Dohasan's Kiowa camp of 176 lodges, and the Indians fled. He moved on to Adobe Walls—the remains of a trading post built by William Bent a score of years earlier. With his horses penned inside the ruins for safekeeping, about 10 a.m. Carson ordered his two howitzers fired, saying, "Pettis, throw a few shell into that crowd over thar." The Indians scattered, and Carson thought they would disperse, but to his surprise about a thousand braves attacked. He moved part of his command inside the walls; the trading post had consisted of one building, about 80 feet square and with a single entrance. When Carson realized that he faced perhaps 3,000 Comanche, Kiowa, Cheyenne, Arapaho, and Kiowa-Apache braves armed with rifles, he decided to withdraw. Pulling back under cover of the howitzers, Carson burned Dohasan's village about dusk. There was no fighting on the following day, and on Sunday morning, November 27, Carson ordered a retreat to New Mexico. Two soldiers and one Ute scout were dead and 15 were wounded. He reported the losses of the hostiles to be 60 killed, 150 wounded, and many lodges destroyed; he was of the opinion that the Indians "acted with more daring and bravery than I have ever witnessed."

Carson's troops reached Fort Bascom on December 20. The First Battle of Adobe Walls was the largest Indian fight of the Civil War and perhaps—in terms of the number of participants—the largest ever, since estimates of the hostiles' strength ranged as high as 7,000 warriors. Kit Carson was a brigadier general when he died in 1868.

Kit Carson became famous through accompanying John C. Frémont on his western explorations. He commanded U. S. Army troops at the First Battle of Adobe Walls and was a brigadier general at his death not long after the end of the Civil War.

Billy Dixon Shot an Indian at Adobe Walls

Billy Dixon, West Virginia-born and orphaned young, was hunting buffalo in Kansas when he was 19; cowhides sold for $1 and bullhides for $2. Because of scarcity produced by the slaughter, in 1872 the hide of a bull was worth $4. Dixon and the other hunters moved southward as the herds diminished, provoking the plains tribes because of the reduced numbers of buffalo and the hunters' violation of the boundary declared by the Treaty of Medicine Lodge; whites were to remain north of the Arkansas River, but by 1874 it was apparent that hunters would have to cross that river to find buffalo in significant numbers. That spring Billy Dixon, some other hunters, and a few Dodge City businessmen chose a spot on East Adobe Walls Creek in present Hutchinson County, Texas. There Myers and Leonard erected a picket building for their store and James Hanrahan built a twenty-by-sixty-foot sod-house saloon. Rath and Wright, of Dodge City, would carry on their hide business in another sod building. Thomas O'Keefe's blacksmith shop was made of pickets.

As the community at Adobe Walls was taking shape a Quahadi medicine man was assuring Quanah Parker that the time had come to expel the whites from the country below the Arkansas River. Already some of the hunters had been killed in the Panhandle. Quanah prepared to attack Adobe Walls before dawn on June 27, 1874. Fortunately for the 28 men and one woman—Mrs. William Olds and her husband were to operate a restaurant in the Rath & Wright store—at about 2 a.m. the ridge pole of Hanrahan's Saloon snapped as if it were collapsing. Bartender Oscar Shepherd and Mike Welch were awakened, and they roused a dozen others to help make repairs; men had been suffocated under sod roofs that had caved in. As they finished bracing the rafters about dawn suddenly they discovered that they were surrounded by Indians preparing an attack.

Billy Dixon wrote:

> There was never a more splendidly barbaric sight. In after years I was glad that I had seen it. Hundreds of warriors, the flower of the fighting men of the southwestern Plains tribes, mounted upon their finest horses, armed with guns and lances, and carrying heavy shields of thick buffalo hide, were coming like the wind. Over all was splashed the rich colors of red, vermillion and ochre, on the bodies of the men, on the bodies of the running horses. Scalps dangled from bridles, gorgeous war-bonnets fluttered their plumes, bright feathers dangled from the tails and manes of the horses, and the bronzed, half-naked bodies of the riders glittered with ornaments of silver and brass. Behind this head-long charging host stretched the Plains, on whose horizon the rising sun was lifting its morning fires.

Dixon made it to Hanrahan's Saloon, where Bat Masterson and seven others had taken refuge. Eleven men were inside Myers and Leonard's Store; Mrs. Olds and the others were at Rath and Wright's. Dixon noted that, "Some of the men were still undressed, but nobody wasted any time hunting his clothes, and many of the men fought for their lives all that summer day barefoot and in their drawers and undershirts."

Billy Dixon, left, was a young buffalo hunter whose celebrated shot at the Second Battle of Adobe Walls brought that Indian fight to a conclusion.

The attacking Kiowa, Comanche, Cheyenne, Arapaho, and Kiowa-Apache numbered from 700 to 1,000. They killed Billy Tyler and Mike and Charlie Shadler, who were sleeping in their wagon; the Shadler brothers and their Newfoundland dog were scalped. The defenders' buffalo guns forced the Indians to pull back out of range; the big Sharp's 50-caliber rifles were accurate at great distances and took a heavy toll of Indians as the sporadic attacks continued all day. Just after Quanah Parker's horse was shot from under him another bullet hit him in the shoulder. To cut off escape Quanah had ordered the whites' mounts killed, with the result that, "We counted fifty-six dead horses scattered in the immediate vicinity of the buildings....Added to this slaughter were the twenty-eight head of oxen that belonged to the Shadler brothers."

On the second day there was no attack. As the war party held its distance some hunters arrived at the trading post. One newcomer furnished a horse, enabling Henry Lease to go to Dodge City for help.

Billy Dixon made his famous shot on the third day. The defenders could see a party of about 15 Indians on a bluff east of them and "some of the boys suggested that I try the big '50' on them....I took careful aim and pulled the trigger. We saw an Indian fall from his horse." Years later D.B. Stribling, the Robertson County Surveyor, measured the distance of the shot and found it to be 1,538 yards.

Hunters kept drifting in, and there were nearly a hundred men present at Adobe Walls by the fifth day. William Olds, the last white casualty, was hurrying down from the lookout box on top of Rath's store—someone had given an alarm, which turned out to be false—and his gun accidentally discharged and killed him.

Most writers have believed the Indians' withdrawal resulted from Dixon's marksmanship. Apparently the chiefs realized they could not prevail over such range and accuracy. After giving up the attack on Adobe Walls, they raided into New Mexico, Colorado, Kansas and Texas and killed about 190 whites. Dixon thought that "the Indians probably came to the conclusion that if they remained long enough, charged often enough and got close enough, all of them would be killed, as they were unable to dislodge us from the buildings." At least fifteen Indians died.

As to the collapsing ridge pole, which had awakened Welch and Shepherd, no one could ever find anything wrong with it. Dixon wrote:

> Every hunter that came in after the fight, as well as every man at the Walls, examined that cottonwood ridge log over and over to find the break, but it could not be found. The two men who were sleeping in the building declared that the noise sounded like the report of a rifle.

The Second Battle of Adobe Walls ended buffalo-hunting in that neighborhood, and Dixon remembered that, "This was the last buffalo-hunting I ever did as a business." The buildings were abandoned, and after a few weeks the Indians returned but took none of the provisions and supplies which remained, evidently believing them to be poisoned.

Dixon scouted for General Nelson Miles from August, 1874, to February, 1883, when he settled on three sections, which included the original Adobe Walls site on Bents Creek. He married in 1894 and moved away from Hutchinson County in 1902. He died March 9, 1913, and was buried near the place where Myers and Leonard had their store at Adobe Walls.

The marker at the left memorializes the Indians who died in the Second Battle of Adobe Walls. The pipe enclosure in the middle is Billy Dixon's grave, and the stone on the right is inscribed with the names of the defenders.

Quanah Parker Was the Last War Chief of the Quahadi Comanche

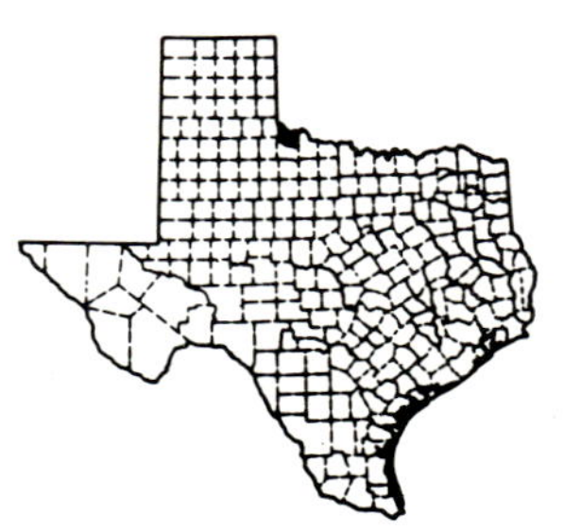

Quanah, whose name meant "fragrant"—or according to another source, "the eagle"—was a son of the white captive, Cynthia Ann Parker, and Peta Nocona. Born in northwest Texas, he was about fifteen years old when his younger sister, Prairie Flower, and his mother were captured by Sul Ross' Rangers on Foard County's Pease River; both died within a few years.

Quanah married first To-ha-yea, a Mescalero Apache for whom he paid five mules. Never happy among the Comanche, she eventually returned to her people. Quanah gave 17 horses for Yellow Bear's daughter, Weckeah.

Both To-ha-yea and Tonarcy were childless, but the other six wives gave Quanah at least 21 sons and daughters. When a white friend would urge that he become monogamous, Quanah would assent on condition that the friend be the one to inform the extra wives that they had to leave. And when Mrs. Lee Hall contended that Quanah should limit himself to one wife he countered with the proposal that he persuade Hall to take additional brides and make Mrs. Hall the "boss wife."

Quanah was present at the Medicine Lodge Council in 1867 but opposed the treaty, which he considered only an old man's settlement forfeiting the young braves' opportunities for glory. The Quahadi—or Antelope—Comanche did not sign this treaty, which forced the Comanche and Kiowa onto a 3-million-acre reservation in what is now southwestern Oklahoma. In his youth Quanah became an important leader and his band was Colonel Ranald Mackenzie's main quarry as he set out to force the hostiles onto the reservation after the Warren Massacre in 1871.

In early 1874 Quanah held a council of Comanche, Kiowa, Cheyenne, and Arapaho in present Kiowa County, Oklahoma, to consider the problem of the white buffalo hunters who had made a headquarters at Adobe Walls. Little Wolf, or Esa-Tai, a Quahadi medicine man, claimed the Great Spirit had shown him how to make a bullet-proof paint that would let them overcome the whites; he also had power to control the elements and to bring back the buffalo in numbers greater than had ever been seen. Border warfare was resumed in Kansas, Colorado and Texas, and Quanah led nearly a thousand braves against the trading post at Adobe Walls. Failing to surprise Bat Masterson, Billy Dixon and 27 other defenders, and unable to overcome the whites' superior fire power, the Indians decided to withdraw. After another year of pursuit by Mackenzie, Colonel Nelson A. Miles, and others, Quanah and his people went to Fort Sill in June, 1875, and asked that they be allowed to settle on reservation land. The Quahadi were the last of the hostile Plains Indians to surrender; the Comanchería was open to settlement.

On the reservation Quanah advocated leasing grazing rights to whites. He became an adept businessman and was a friend of Burk Burnett, Dan Waggoner, and other cattlemen who ran their herds in North Texas and the Indian Territory. He was their guest at the Fort Worth Fat Stock Show, and through them he met—and went wolf-hunting with—President Theodore Roosevelt. He attended the 1885 New Orleans World's Fair and made several trips to Washington.

Quanah Parker and his wife, Tonarcy, outside their lodge in the Indian Territory.

De Shields' book on Cynthia Ann Parker contains an interesting description of the way Quanah lived in 1886:

> We visited Quanah in his teepee. He is a fine specimen of physical manhood, tall, muscular—as straight as an arrow; gray, look-you-straight-through-the-eyes, very dark skin, perfect teeth, and heavy, raven-black hair—the envy of feminine hearts—he wears hanging in two queues wrapped around with red cloth. His hair is parted in the middle; the scalp-lock, a portion of hair the size of a dollar, plaited and tangled, signifying: "If you want fight you can have it."
>
> Quanah is now camped with a thousand of his subjects at the foot of some hills near Anadarko. Their white teepees and the inmates dressed in their bright blankets and feathers, cattle grazing, children playing, lent a weird charm to the lonely, desolated hills lately devastated by prairie fire.
>
> He has three squaws, his favorite being the daughter of Yellow Bear, who met his death by asphyxiation at Fort Worth in December last. (Quanah and Yellow Bear were spending the night at the Pickwick Hotel, and gas escaping from the extinguished gas light killed Yellow Bear and made Quanah quite sick.) Quanah was attired in a full suit of buckskin tunic, leggings and moccasins elaborately trimmed in beads—a red breech-cloth, with ornamental ends hanging down. A very handsome and expensive Mexican blanket was thrown around his body; in his ears were little stuffed birds....When traveling he assumes a complete civilian's outfit—dude collar, watch and chain—takes out his earrings—he, of course, cannot cut off his long hair, saying that he could no longer be "big chief."

As chiefs died or retired Quanah came to be regarded as head of the Apache and Kiowa, as well as the Comanche. Former Texas Ranger Captain Lee Hall was critical of Quanah. Hall was the Indian agent at Anadarko in the middle eighties, and he said Horseback was the main Comanche chief until his death in 1885 and that Quanah was never more than the "Washington chief," maintained in power by cattlemen who paid much less than they should have for grazing rights. Quanah was presiding judge of the Court of Indian Offenses, and he built a large house with a room for each wife, and large white stars—such as those generals wore—on the red roof. Hall charged that this house was an improper gift of the cattlemen who used him.

Quanah loved to make speeches, particularly at the Hardeman County town which bore his name and which he regarded as belonging to him. He also took a proprietary interest in the Quanah, Acme and Pacific Railway, since his profile was used in its advertising. Upon completion of the railroad, in October, 1910, a great celebration was held at the state fair in Dallas, and Quanah and his family, in full Comanche dress, made the trip by special train. In his address that day he said:

> I used to be a bad man, now I am citizen of the United States. I pay taxes the same as you people do. We are the same people now....The Texas History says General Ross killed my father....He no kill my father. I want to get that in Texas history straight up....no kill my father. He not there.
>
> I hear somebody say something about Quanah. That not good country. All prairie dogs, all snakes. That not so. Quanah town good town. You can raise anything in there. All nice houses in there....

Holding a lance which he called his knife, Quanah continued:

> I fought General Mackenzie. He had 2,000 men. I had 450 men. I used this knife. I see a little further, perhaps 8 miles, lots soldiers coming. I say hold on, no go over there, maybe we go at night, maybe stampede soldiers' horses....I gather maybe 350 United States horses that night. You

Quanah Parker poses with two of his wives, Pi-uuh and Sohnee, on the porch of his star-roofed house in the Indian Territory.

see how bad me at that time. Next morning they come up my trail. I ready to fight. I used this knife....I tell my men to stand up behind hill, holler, shoot and run. I run to one side and used this knife. I come up to right side and killed mans, sergeant and scout. You see how bad I was at that time....

On February 23, 1911, Quanah died. He was buried beside his mother at the Post Oak Mission. His epitaph, written by his daughter, Neda Parker Birdsong, read, "Resting here until day breaks and shadows fail and darkness disappears."

—Western History Collection, University of Oklahoma Library

Quanah Parker was the last war chief of the Quahadi Comanche.

Quanah Parker loved to make speeches—such as this one at Matador—and ride in parades.

As the years passed, the Comanche chief, Quanah, became the spokesman for the Kiowa and other tribes at the Fort Sill reservation, too.

Cynthia Ann Parker Was Reburied in Oklahoma

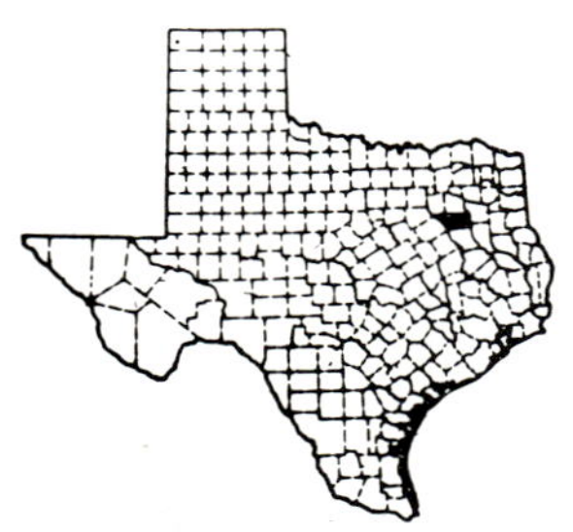

Cynthia Ann Parker, who was carried into captivity by the Comanche when she was nine years old, married Peta Nocona and bore him three children, Quanah, Pecos, and Prairie Flower. She and the infant Prairie Flower were captured by whites on the Pease River in Foard County in 1860, when she was about 33. She was sent to her Parker relatives. Prairie Flower, two years old, did not live long. Cynthia Ann, who had not a drop of Indian blood, longed for her former life with the Comanche. She attempted to hire guides to take her back, explaining that she did not look forward so much to life with Peta Nocona—who was accustomed to kicking her in the ribs—but she simply wanted to return to a way of life that was her own.

The Texas legislature gave her a league of land and a pension to be administered by her brother, Silas Parker, Jr., at whose home in Anderson County she died in 1864. At the 1910 state fair in Dallas Quanah said:

> We moved from Texas over into Oklahoma, my country. Two years ago I been to Washington. I see John Stephens, Congressman from Texas. I tell him would like to get bill, $1,000, to move my mother's remains. Two years ago bill passed and after that somebody, New York bill, stopped that bill and last June I'd been to Washington. I come again, see about it, made bill $800. I used $200 to buy new coffin.
>
> Now ladies and gentlemen, Texas objects to me do that. I have over at home my older son, dead some 7 or 8 years ago. Nobody know when me die, maybe tomorrow or ten years. But me have family graveyard and we want bury my mother there.

In 1910 Quanah's son-in-law, A.C. Birdsong, was sent to Texas to locate Cynthia Ann's body and make arrangements for its removal to Oklahoma. He found her in Henderson County's Fosterville Cemetery and he reported that:

> Upon locating Cynthia Ann's remains I also found proof that the remains of her daughter, Prairie Flower, were in the grave beside her. I had no authority to remove the remains of Prairie Flower but after giving the matter due consideration I decided to put the remains of the mother and daughter together and have them sent to Cache, Oklahoma.

The government appropriation was apparently $200 for removal of the body and $1,000 for a monument. The reburial, at Post Oak Mission near Indiahoma, drew one of the largest crowds in the history of the Comanche country. In addition to the Indians, more than a thousand whites attended. Quanah spoke in Comanche, then in English. Three months later, February 23, 1911, Quanah died and was buried by the side of Cynthia Ann.

After nearly half a century it was necessary to remove both graves because of the expansion of the Fort Sill missile-testing range. The seven living children of Quanah Parker accepted the proposal to rebury him and their grandmother in Fort Sill's post cemetery. Quanah's last surviving widow, Topay, 87 years old, lost her lawsuit to keep his remains out of the military cemetery. Quanah and Cynthia Ann Parker were buried with military honors at Fort Sill on August 9, 1957, a few feet from the graves of the Kiowa Satanta and other plains chiefs.

—Western History Collection, University of Oklahoma Library

Cynthia Ann Parker was disinterred from her Henderson County grave and reburied in Oklahoma's Post Oak Cemetery in 1910. Above, Quanah walks behind the pallbearers and beside the little girl in the plaid dress. He died in the following year.

Charlie Goodnight Pioneered the Panhandle

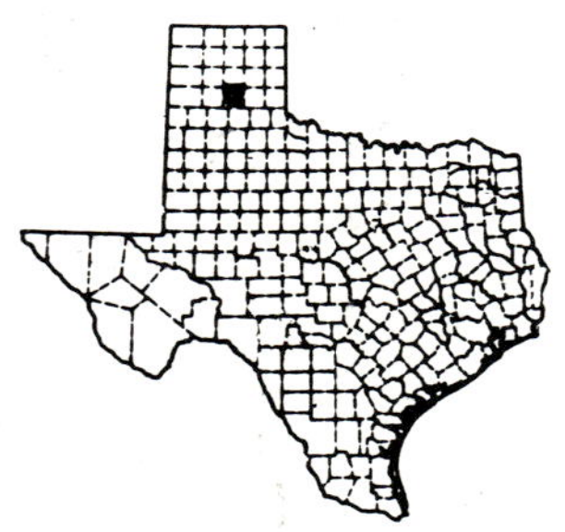

A few months after Quanah Parker led his Quahadi Comanche onto the reservation at Fort Sill, Charles Goodnight brought 1,600 cattle onto the Staked Plains of Texas. After spending the summer of 1876 on the Canadian River he moved south to the Palo Duro Canyon, where he established a ranch on the Prairie Dog Town Fork of Red River. As Goodnight took the herd into the canyon it was necessary to evict earlier occupants, some 10,000 buffalo. At first cowhands riding herd not only held the cattle in the canyon but kept the buffalo out. Three hundred miles beyond the frontier, in present Randall, Armstrong, Briscoe and Swisher counties, the Palo Duro Canyon is more than 100 miles long and 1,100 feet deep. The width varies from fifteen miles in some places to a few hundred yards in others. In a country lacking timber for fencing the canyon offered confinement for the herds as well as some protection from the weather. The Comancheros and the Comanche used it as a market place; Coronado may have camped there in 1541. General Ranald Mackenzie, in perhaps West Texas' most significant Indian battle, defeated the Comanche there in 1874. Goodnight was the Panhandle's first rancher, preceding Thomas Sherman Bugbee by only a few weeks. Until his arrival only Casimero Romero and a few other New Mexico sheepmen lived in the Panhandle.

Born in Illinois the day before the Alamo fell, March 5, 1836, Goodnight came to Milam County, Texas, when he was ten years old. He moved to Palo Pinto County in 1857 and learned the country while doing ranger service. Goodnight was scouting for Sul Ross when Cynthia Ann Parker was recovered in the battle of the Pease River in present Foard County. At the age of nine—in the year of Goodnight's birth—she was carried into captivity by a Comanche war party at Fort Parker, Limestone County.

Goodnight served with a frontier regiment during the Civil War and then became the partner of Oliver Loving, who was one of the first men to trail cattle out of Texas; they blazed the Goodnight-Loving Trail from Fort Belknap, Young County, by way of the Horsehead Crossing and Fort Sumner, New Mexico, to Colorado in 1866. Loving was wounded by a Comanche and died at Fort Sumner, New Mexico, the following year after making Goodnight promise to bury him in Weatherford. Later Goodnight wrote, "He was the nearest thing to a father to me that I have ever known."

Goodnight had laid out the Goodnight Trail from Fort Sumner to Cheyenne, Wyoming, and was ranching near Pueblo, Colorado, when he decided to move to the Panhandle. J. Evetts Haley, in his splendid *Charles Goodnight, Cowman and Plainsman*, described the isolation of the Palo Duro:

A hundred miles toward Kansas, Jim Cator had a buffalo camp on the North Palo Duro; about a hundred miles to the east and a little north, Fort Elliott was staked out on the Sweetwater; Fort Griffin lay a much longer journey southwest, and the nearest settlements in New Mexico, Kansas, and Colorado were from two hundred to two hundred and fifty miles away.

Mrs. Goodnight, living in the dugout ranch headquarters on the floor of the

The long life of Charlie Goodnight covered the period from the Texas revolution to the beginning of the great depression.

canyon, had little companionship. Her nearest neighbor was 75 miles away and the closest settlement was 200 miles. Haley wrote:

> The solitude and the wind were trying for a woman, and it was quite a domestic blessing when one day a cowboy rode in with three chickens in a sack. "No one can ever know how much pleasure and company they were to me," Mrs. Goodnight once said. "They were something I could talk to, they would run to me when I called them and follow me everywhere I went. They knew me and tried to talk to me in their language."

Goodnight told a reporter, "I didn't own a foot of land when I trailed my cattle down from Colorado....I had no money then." Needing capital to develop the ranch, he formed a partnership with John Adair, an Englishman, in 1877; thus the JA—Adair's initials—Ranch was begun. Under Goodnight's management—and Adair visited the Panhandle only three times—the ranch grew to mammoth proportions; more than 100,000 cattle grazed 1.3 million acres. Adair died in 1885 and two years later Goodnight and Mrs. Adair divided the assets of the partnership; he received the 140,000-acre Quitaque Ranch and 20,000 cattle in satisfaction of his one-third interest in the JA. Goodnight sold the Quitaque in 1890 and bought 160 sections at Goodnight, Armstrong County. Later he sold this ranch on condition that he might live out his days there.

In February or March of 1878 one of the hands brought word that Indians were coming in large numbers. Goodnight said, "I at once mounted a horse and started to meet them....The Indians were killing cattle at a fearful rate....I told Quanah I wanted him at headquarters, some ten miles up the canyon, for the purpose of making a treaty...." The next day a bargain was made whereby Goodnight would donate two beeves a day while the Indians searched for buffalo; Goodnight was stalling while awaiting the arrival of Fort Elliott soldiers to return the Comanche to the reservation.

The first cattle Goodnight brought to the Panhandle were Durhams. Because the canyon effectively confined the stock he was able to keep his best animals segregated and to begin upgrading his herd. Buying more blooded stock he developed animals with the toughness of the old Texas cattle and the size and shape of the dominant Herefords. But he never lost his affection and admiration for Old Blue, a longhorn John Chisum sold him in a lot of 5,000 steers; because Old Blue always worked his way to the front of the herd Goodnight recognized his leadership qualities and did not sell him. The six-year-old Blue led Goodnight's cattle from Colorado to the Staked Plains, and on drives to Dodge City the other steers followed the sound of the bell he wore; the clapper was muffled at night, but each morning he would stand at the head of the herd, wait for the bell to be cleared, and then head north. For eight years Blue practiced his calling. Aware of his importance he bedded down with the saddle horses and visited the chuck wagon for treats, which he considered his due. Goodnight believed him to be worth a dozen hands. He died of old age in 1890, and his horns are on display at Canyon's Panhandle-Plains Historical Museum.

Along the way Goodnight experimented with the cattalo—a cross between buffalo and cattle—but finally he decided it was too expensive. His interest in the buffalo did not wane; for half a century he kept about 250 head. On several occasions Indians came down from the Comanche reservation, got Goodnight's permission, and killed a buffalo in memory of other times.

At first the Panhandle counties' legal business was conducted at Gainesville, Henrietta, or some other distant county seat. After a district court was established for Wheeler County in 1880 the most convenient route for the judge was to go by train

This replica of Charlie Goodnight's dugout home and ranch headquarters is situated in Palo Duro Canyon.

from Denton to Kansas and then to take stagecoaches down to Mobeetie, an 800-mile journey, although Denton was only 300 miles away by crow-flight. Charles Goodnight was the first president of the Panhandle Stock Association, which was organized to protect area cowmen from rustlers, South Texas cattle carrying the tick fever so lethal to local stock, and cattle driven by the north wind onto Panhandle grass. The organization hired inspectors and detectives to catch rustlers, forced herds from lower and warmer parts of the state to skirt the Panhandle, and sponsored construction of a great drift fence. The *Dodge City Times* of November 6, 1884, announced:

> The longest line of fencing in the world will be the wire fence extending from Indian Territory west across the Texas Pan-Handle and thirty-five miles into New Mexico. The total length being 200 miles....Its course will be the line of the Canadian river and its purpose is to stop the drift of the northern cattle.

During a blizzard, an earlier drift fence halted so many antelope that Clarendon settlers killed 1,500 of them.

Mr. and Mrs. Goodnight founded Goodnight College in 1898; the Baptists took over its management in 1905, at which time a faculty of six taught 175 students. The peak enrollment was 250; room and board for a 4½ month term was $55.25. In 1913 the school became a junior college, and it closed at the beginning of World War I.

Mrs. Goodnight died in 1926, and he then married Corinne Goodnight; he was 91 and she was in her twenties. Charles Goodnight died at his winter home in Arizona on December 12, 1929.

From a high point in Armstrong County near Goodnight, Texas, the graves of Charles and Mary Goodnight overlook the surrounding country.

Goodnight's admiration for the buffalo caused him to try to incorporate their qualities into his herd. His cattalo experiment was finally abandoned because it was too costly.

For many years Charlie Goodnight maintained a herd of about 250 buffalo on his ranch.

Tascosa Was the Panhandle's Cowboy Capital

When Charles Goodnight arrived, the only residents of the Panhandle were a few sheepherders from eastern New Mexico living on the Canadian River. One of these, Casimero Romero, in 1876 settled his family and several thousand sheep at an ancient Indian campsite where Atascosa Creek joined the Canadian. There, near an easy crossing, Tascosa would come into existence and show signs of becoming the great city of the Panhandle. Instead, technology would kill it, as bridges made the good ford inconsequential, railroads generated rival towns, and barbed wire fences made it difficult to get to Tascosa.

Goodnight stopped there briefly, then agreed to take his cattle to Palo Duro Canyon and leave the Canadian to Romero. But other cowmen came to stay, making Tascosa the capital of a booming cattle kingdom which included the LX, LS, XIT, Frying Pan, and LIT ranches. An application for a post office was denied since there was already an Atascosa, Texas, so the first "a" was dropped, and, in 1878, Julius Howard became Tascosa's first postmaster.

In the next year the first Panhandle county, Wheeler, was organized, with its capital at Mobeetie; local pride precipitated efforts to organize Oldham County, which was then supervised from Mobeetie, so Wheeler County commissioners, in 1880, ordered an election to choose officials and a county seat for Oldham. The Canadian settlement was in two parts; Romero supported Lower Tascosa, while ranchers and merchants campaigned for Upper Tascosa and won. Cape B. Willingham was elected sheriff, and an interpreter had to be appointed because half the commissioners court spoke Spanish.

Because of continuing disorders in Lincoln County, New Mexico, John Chisum moved his herds to the Tascosa vicinity. The new town also attracted his former employee, William Bonney; in 1878 he was an 18-year-old, buck-toothed killer called Billy the Kid; since there was then no local government the cattlemen held a public meeting to tell Bonney he might stay in Tascosa only on good behavior. After several months Bonney moved to Portales, New Mexico, and continued rustling Texas cattle. The Panhandle Cattlemen's Association, founded in 1880, sent agents after Bonney's gang. About the same time, Lincoln County sheriff Pat Garrett, formerly of Tascosa, was ordered to retire Bonney. With the help of cowboys hired by Panhandle ranchers, Garrett captured Bonney and turned him over to the authorities in Santa Fé. After he shot two guards and escaped, Bonney was killed by Pat Garrett at Fort Sumner in July of 1881.

After Sheriff Willingham shot a cowhand, in 1879, the Tascosans decided they should have a boothill cemetery; Dodge City, Kansas—240 miles away, but the metropolis of the plains—had one in which eight rowdies had been planted before the town was a year old. Among those who died with their boots on and were buried in Tascosa were: "Norwood, killed by Maley; Maley, killed by Frank Norwood's brother, Ed; the Dutchman, killed by the Catfish Kid; and Bacilio Sanches, killed by a horse."

Joseph Glidden, the inventor of barbed wire, and Henry Sanborn had started the

A bunch of cowboys from the LS Ranch arrive in downtown Tascosa.

Frying Pan Ranch to demonstrate the wire. In 1882 they fenced the first pasture in the Panhandle. The 200-mile north plains drift fence was built after a few months to keep cattle from straying into the Panhandle. In time the proliferation of fences made Tascosa inaccessible and ended the trail drives which were so important to the local economy; however, residents counted on the railroad to make Tascosa a great city.

The Fort Worth and Denver was laying track, and when C.F. Rudolph began publishing the *Pioneer*, in 1886, he believed it would have to come through Tascosa. The future looked bright. Tascosa had seven saloons, and the dance-hall girls included Rocking Chair Emma, Santa Fe Mol, Mustang Mae, Spotted Jack, and Ole Buck. Nine other counties were governed from Tascosa; court was held twice a year by Judge Frank Willis and District Attorney Temple Houston, who also served the other two organized Panhandle counties, Wheeler (Mobeetie) and Donley (Clarendon). Houston, the youngest son of Texas' first president, once bested Billy the Kid and Bat Masterson in a Tascosa shooting contest.

Back numbers of the Tascosa *Pioneer* gave an invaluable view of life there:

> It is reported...that the wild horses are on the plains out north of here in about their usual numbers but that they are decidedly wild and hard to capture....Considerable preparations have been and are being made for the Christmas tree Friday night, which is to be at the courthouse....The chicken thief is abroad in the land....Great is the Fort Worth, Denver and Tascosa railway....Tascosa has a population of some four hundred....Lee Howard came in the first of the week with a load of buffalo meat....The dentist will be in town Friday.

A Catholic mission was begun in 1889, but Tascosa never had a church or a resident pastor or priest. Sporadically, schools opened and died for lack of nourishment. Businessmen were unable to raise the subsidy the railroad demanded for coming through Tascosa, so the depot was located a mile or so from town. Of more importance was the fact that the railroad had generated too many rivals. Residents moved away, and stores closed as business declined. A flood of the Canadian destroyed many of the buildings. In 1916 the priest serving St. Barnabas mission wrote, "Town gone. County seat transferred to Vega. All Catholics gone."

Cowhands—the real item—hoist a few at a Tascosa establishment.

Cal Farley's Boys Ranch, present occupant of the Tascosa townsite, keeps this longhorn as a reminder of the cattle kingdom.

Since Dodge City had a boothill for those who died violently, proud Tascosa had to have one, too.

The Salt War Occurred at San Elizario

The settlements at the Pass of the North were still quite isolated from the rest of Texas in 1877; it was at least 500 miles to any other place of consequence and Austin, the capital, was 600 miles away. The people of the Upper Río Grande Valley lived much as they had prior to Texas independence, four decades before, when the Río Grande was the artery serving a single people scattered along both banks. The river could be forded eight months of the year; families lived north and south of the stream and could wade back and forth at will. Towns grew up in pairs. The fact that the Great River of the North had become an international boundary was of no consequence to those who crossed it to visit kinsmen.

In 1877, the largest of the towns was still Paso del Norte, which was soon to become Juárez. Franklin, present El Paso, had only 800 people, about the same number as Socorro; both were smaller than Ysleta, the county seat, and San Elizario, whose population was 2,000. Fewer than a hundred El Paso County residents were not of Mexican extraction. They were German, Canadian, English, Irish, and Jewish, lived mainly in Franklin, held most of the local offices, and were resented by the majority, whose loyalties were to Mexico.

From earliest times the people of northern Mexico and the Pass had hauled salt—free to all takers—from area deposits; most recently they had used salt lakes at the foot of the Guadalupe Mountains ninety miles east of San Elizario; the haulers of salt had built a road for that purpose. Since no water was available during the two-day and two-night journey, they left San Elizario fully laden with water, some of the barrels to be dropped off midway for use on the return trip. There was always a market for salt; in fact, it was one of the area's few dependable sources of income, perhaps the only hope of a farmer whose crops were lost to drouth or disease.

The Salt War began when attempts were made to charge the haulers. Samuel Maverick, of San Antonio, filed a claim on 1,280 acres of the deposits, arousing little opposition, for plenty of salt remained outside the claim; however, there was some resentment of Maverick's possible use of the haulers' road.

In 1868 Republican boss W.W. Mills and others, who were called the Salt Ring, tried to obtain title to the deposits outside the Maverick claim. They were unsuccessful but provoked the formation of an opposition group headed by Mills' former ally, A.J. Fountain. Fountain defeated Mills for a state senate seat. Although Father Antonio Borajo, of San Elizario parish, had urged Fountain to obtain the salt lakes—so they could divide the fees, which the priest would advise his parishioners to pay—Fountain wanted El Paso County to own the deposits. Borajo thwarted him by telling the people that the county ownership would make it impossible for salt to be taken by their kinsmen from below the border. After many troubles—including gunplay and litigation—in 1875 Fountain moved to New Mexico.

During the Salt War crowds filled this sleepy San Elizario street, where later Billy the Kid
extricated a comrade from the old adobe jail on the left.

Aware of the waning of Republican strength, Democrat Charles Howard had moved to San Elizario in 1872. He was elected district attorney, and two years later his friend, Louis Cardis, a former officer in Garibaldi's army, was sent to the legislature. Cardis and Father Borajo, both Italians, were good friends who controlled the Mexican-American vote; they became Howard's enemies after he was appointed district judge; Howard claimed they were again demanding a salt monopoly. Cardis blocked Howard's service in the constitutional convention and caused him to lose his judgeship in 1876. Howard thrashed Cardis twice, in Austin and San Antonio. Father Borajo, ordered to Mexico, actually departed San Elizario only after his bishop came in person to oust him and after Borajo denounced his superior and fellow priests as Protestants and thieves.

In the meantime Howard had bought Maverick's claim and acquired title to the rest of the salt deposits in the name of his father-in-law. After Howard warned that no salt might be taken without payment, two San Elizario men, José Juárez and Macedonia Gándara, defied him, and Howard had them arrested. Learning that a mob planned to kill him. Howard stayed one night at Ysleta with Sheriff Charles Kerber. The next morning the sheriff's house was surrounded by a mob which took Howard to San Elizario. For three days his captors demanded that Howard give a bond pledging not to prosecute them and promising to leave the county and allow the courts to decide the salt question; finally he acquiesced and was released. His sureties on the bond were Charles Ellis, John Atkinson, Jesús Cobos, and Tomás García, all of San Elizario. From Mesilla, New Mexico, on October 6, Howard informed the Texas governor, by telegraph, that a Mexican invasion was imminent. In fact, there had been much political turmoil, Indian troubles, and drouth in Chihuahua, which made the availability of salt especially important.

On October 7 Howard returned to Franklin (El Paso) with an army escort from Fort Bayard; Fort Bliss had not been garrisoned for several months. On October 10 Howard killed Cardis in Joseph Schutz's store and fled to New Mexico. Terrified of the reaction of the Mexican-American majority, Schutz wired General Edward Hatch, "...we are expecting a terrible catastrophe in the county, as threats have been made that every American would be killed if harm came to Cardis." Schutz signed his name and "the citizens of Franklin, Tex."

The first outside help to arrive was Ranger major John B. Jones, who had gotten there as quickly as possible by riding the train from Austin to Topeka, Kansas, and then to Santa Fé, New Mexico, where he caught a stage for Franklin. Jones stopped in Mesilla, New Mexico, long enough to talk to Howard and Fountain and reached Franklin on November 7. The mob had declared Howard's bond forfeited and his sureties liable because of his return to the county and his murder of Cardis. Jones met with the mob leaders; he raised a detachment of Rangers, made John B. Tays the commander, and sent them to San Elizario. When Howard returned to Franklin, Jones arrested him. On November 17 he was arraigned for the Cardis killing and released on $4,000 bond. Matters became less tense, for a main concern of the mob had been that Howard would not be prosecuted. Jones left for Austin on November 22, 1877. The trouble appeared to be over until a caravan headed for the salt lakes and Howard's agent, J. E. McBride, who was also one of the Rangers on

During the Salt War the besieged Rangers had their headquarters at the site of this building. In the background is the San Elizario church.

duty at San Elizario, notified his employer. On December 12, Howard arrived in San Elizario to enforce his prohibition against the hauling of salt without payment. (Father Borajo's successor at San Elizario had written earlier, "Three-fourths of these fellows are already starving in consequence of their bad crops and are determined to get something from the salt or fight to the death.")

The Rangers were in an adobe house near the crossing of the Ysleta road and the Main street of the town. Diagonally across the intersection was the Charles Ellis store and John Atkinson's home. Howard was staying at the Ellis house that night, but he came to Ranger headquarters about midnight and reported Ellis missing. Ellis had gone out to reason with the mob; when next seen, two days later, he had been stabbed in the heart, his throat had been cut, and he had been scalped.

The leader of the mob was Chico Barela, Cardis' good friend. The commander of troops sent earlier from Fort Bayard, a Captain Blair, came from Franklin in response to Tays' summons but decided, after talking to Barela, that none of the mob was from Mexico and refused to help. Had he intervened the disorders probably would have ended; the mob interpreted his failure as approval of its actions.

At daybreak the mob began firing upon the defenders in the Rangers' adobe and in the Ellis store. Sergeant C. E. Mortimer was killed that afternoon while on patrol between the store and Atkinson's house. Firing and looting continued all day; Miguel García was killed while protecting the Ellis store. The mob consisted of about 350 local residents and an equal number from across the river. A witness wrote, "The leaders of the mob were all ignorant men. Chico Barela cannot tell the first letter of his name and he is the most intelligent among them."

The siege lasted from Wednesday until the next Monday when the leaders of the mob promised that if Howard surrendered and relinquished his claim to the salt lakes everyone could depart in peace. Howard gave up and was taken to the mob's headquarters. John Atkinson followed to serve as an interpreter, bringing along $11,000 to satisfy the defaulted bond. After the Rangers had surrendered and were locked up, Howard was marched outside, shot by five men from below the Río Grande and hacked apart with a machette. In spite of Barela's protests, Atkinson and John McBride were shot, apparently by order of Father Borajo. Their bodies were thrown into a well while the mob fell to looting stores and homes. Tays' Rangers were saved by Barela's threats to fire on anyone trying to harm them. One witness wrote of the looting:

> ...wagon-load after wagon-load of plunder was hauled away from the town to the opposite side of the river. Doña Teodora, the widow of Ellis, was robbed of her jewelry, dresses, bed-clothes, furniture, everything; her house was stripped.

Gregorio García, who was later the mayor of San Elizario, was one of the nine men in the Ellis store; there were about a dozen in the Ranger headquarters. Of the executions he said:

> Howard and McBride went first—I saw both of them shot. The brave one was Atkinson. When he was stood against the wall he told the mob he would give the word to fire. He spoke excellent Spanish and told the mob to fire at his heart. When he said fire,

On the ground where a mob lynched Howard, McBride and Atkinson a hundred years ago, the San Elizario football team attends to such gentler pursuits as scalping the Fort Davis Indians.

five bullets struck him in the stomach and he shouted, "Mas arriba." (Higher up, you——). Two shots rang out, and Atkinson crumpled to the ground—struck in the head.

Later, General Hatch, with units from forts Bayard and Davis, arrived to establish order. (The troops sent earlier had kept out of harm's way. Upon returning from San Elizario, Tays said he found the soldiers ready to come to his aid "sometime next spring.") The sheriff, with "a posse of hard characters," as C. L. Sonnichsen put it, "marched to San Elizario, committing rape and murder enroute, and camped there till Christmas, quarrelling among themselves and shooting each other when no better prospects for homicide were available."

No one was ever punished for the murders; the haulers paid agents of Howard's father-in-law for the salt they took; and the findings of a congressional investigation brought about the reestablishment of Fort Bliss.

In this peaceful square, 98 years ago, angry haulers of salt from deposits near Guadalupe Peak rioted and lynched Judge Charles Howard and others. Los Portales, where El Paso County's first school was held, is in the background.

Jefferson Davis Was to be A & M's First President

Jefferson Davis' initial affiliation with Texas was as a young Mississippi congressman supporting annexation. A West Pointer and former son-in-law of General Zachary Taylor, Davis believed Texas had been part of the United States in 1819 and was given erroneously to Spain by the Adams-Onis Treaty, which defined the boundary. Davis left Congress when the Mexican War began, and as colonel of the Mississippi Rifles he reached Port Isabel, Texas, in August of 1845. After a brief training period he served under General Taylor in Mexico. As Franklin Pierce's Secretary of War, Davis imported camels into Texas to test their utility as freight haulers to the Pacific. The experiment was a success, but the slavery controversy prevented establishment of regular camel transport between Texas and California.

Davis, as Confederate president, appointed Texan John Reagan Postmaster General and made Governor Francis Lubbock his chief aide; both were with him when he was captured at the close of the war. Since General Robert E. Lee had been president of Washington College, there was precedent for Texans inviting Davis to head their new agricultural and mechanical college.

The Morrill Act, signed into law by President Abraham Lincoln in 1862, provided for the endowment of colleges to teach agriculture and the mechanical arts in the several states. Texas was not in the Union when the land grant legislation was passed, but in 1871 Governor E.J. Davis urged legislators to establish an institution to take advantage of the act. Funds were appropriated, and the commission appointed to choose a site selected some 2,400 acres on the railroad in Brazos County, which was in the center of the state's population. The first board of directors did not meet until the summer of 1875, when Jefferson Davis was elected president of the college and offered a salary of $4,000 a year.

Davis stated later, "When I was asked to accept...I consented....I think Texas is a great and most wonderful state. It is destined to be the most useful, the most necessary, and the most important of all the States in the Union." But Davis' family and friends thought his duties at the new college would be too arduous, and he "finally yielded and declined the presidency with regret."

The board then appointed T.S. Gathright, who had been recommended by Davis. When the college opened the enrollment was 107 and there were six professors. The mechanical arts teacher had no degree, and the agriculture professor was a minister. There was practically no agricultural instruction for the very good reason that some knowledge of Texas farming had to be developed before it could be taught. There were no books on the subject; instruction had to be based upon research done in Illinois and Wisconsin, where soils and climates differed from those in Texas. A student noted that the only agricultural education he obtained "was from a botanizing expedition from which he learned to classify tumbleweed."

President Gathright corresponded weekly with Jefferson Davis. He objected to the Morrill Act's military training requirements, and chronic dissension caused the board to ask that the entire faculty resign. In 1879 Gathright's successor, James Garland James, hired the staff of Austin's Texas Military Institute to replace the departed professors.

The A & M cadet corp prepares for inspection. Their uniforms resemble those officially prescribed for soldiers of the late Confederacy.

Sul Ross Made A & M a Going Concern

The future of Texas A & M was in doubt until Lawrence Sullivan Ross became its president. Ross—a genuine hero, a man of action, and a learned man—was idolized throughout the state; at the same time his demeanor was quite ordinary. The *Henderson Times* reported:

> Almost any evening can be seen the governor of the greatest state in the Union, sitting out of doors, in front of the temporary capitol, surrounded by Dick, Tom and Harry, discussing the current events, or indulging in anecdotes....Ross is a pure specimen of democracy.

Sul Ross, born in Iowa in 1838, was brought to Milam County, Texas, when he was a year old. His father, Shapley Prince Ross, was an Indian fighter, a Ranger captain, and builder of the first house in Waco. He operated the ferry across the Brazos; his daughter, Kate, was the first white child born in Waco; and he was the agent for the Brazos Indian Reservation in the fifties. Young Sul Ross got his initial Indian experience while commanding a company of reservation scouts on Major Earl Van Dorn's Wichita Expedition; Ross was badly wounded, but he recovered a captive, of whom he later wrote:

> On the 28th of October, 1858, I had a battle with the Comanches at Wichita Mts. and there recaptured a little white girl about eight years old, whose parentage, nor indeed any trace of her kindred, was ever found. I adopted, reared and educated her, giving her the name of Lizzie Ross; the former name being in honor of the young lady—Lizzie Tinsley—to whom I was then engaged and afterwards married in May 1861....She married a wealthy merchant of California, had one son as a result of the union, but both died in 1886 leaving no trace of race or lineage.

After recovering from his wound and graduating from Alabama's Wesleyan University, in the fall of 1860 the 21-year-old Sul Ross was appointed captain of Rangers by Governor Sam Houston. He was ordered to raise a company of 60 men for frontier duty; Indian depredations were worse than they had ever been. On December 19, Ross and 47 Rangers, scout Charles Goodnight, two dozen soldiers, and Jack Cureton's 70-man company of volunteers were following the path of a war party when they came upon a band of Comanche breaking camp on the Pease River in present Foard County. The rangers and soldiers charged the surprised Indians. In a brief battle Ross wounded the leader and ordered him to surrender.

> He refused and walking back to a small tree began to chant a wild, weird war song, when a young Mexican shot him dead. I took his shield, lance, bows and arrows and beautiful headdress of eagle feathers as trophies.

Goodnight then noticed that a captured squaw had blue eyes and blonde hair. Goodnight thought her obvious grief caused Ross to believe, erroneously, that the dead chief was her husband, Peta Nocona. Someone suggested that the squaw might be Cynthia Ann Parker, and a few days later Isaac Parker came to see if she might be his

Lawrence Sullivan Ross fought in 135 battles and had five horses shot out from under him. At 25 he was a Confederate brigadier general.

missing niece. When the name, Cynthia Ann, was mentioned the Indian woman showed signs of recognition, and after Colonel Parker repeated it she stood, patted herself, and said, "Me Cincee Ann."

When the Civil War began, Ross joined his brother's company as a private, but on December 21, 1863, at the age of 25, Ross became a Confederate brigadier general. Ross' Texas Brigade, according to the *Dallas Herald*, had 4,700 men when it crossed the Mississippi River in May, 1862; three years and 235 engagements later its strength was only 600, although only 150 had deserted or joined other commands. Ross participated in 135 battles and had five horses shot out from under him.

Back in McLennan County after the war—and broke—Ross began farming, but in late 1873, after lawlessness forced two sheriffs to resign, Ross was elected to that office. He was an effective sheriff, a delegate to the 1875 constitutional convention, and a state senator at the time the capitol burned in 1881. Ross was elected governor—as Jim Hogg became attorney general—in 1886. (Originally Ross' Texas Brigade had been commanded by General Joseph Hogg, the attorney general's father.) Ross had two rather quiet administrations during which mental institutions were established at San Antonio and Terrell, a boys' reformatory opened at Gatesville, and a state orphanage was founded at Corsicana. Fort Worth editor B.B. Paddock described the Ross incumbency as "the most universally approved of any administration prior to or since that time." The new capitol was dedicated in May, 1888, before a crowd of 9,000, which included three former governors and General Mexia of Mexico; Ross, "with all the pride of an old Texan and of presiding at the head of the government on this grand occasion and with a countenance beaming with the delightful conception of it delivered an eloquent and feeling address." The main speaker was Temple Houston, the youngest son of the first president.

Governor Ross had been interested in Texas A & M since its inception. The college still had not gotten on its feet, although the cost was only $250 a year for everything, including uniforms, and the education was as good as might be had anywhere in Texas. But farmers scoffed at the idea that agriculture could be taught in classrooms; such an effort was "Yankee silliness." Others accused A & M of being a "nest for a military aristocracy," and some of those parents who approved of its martial flavor sent their incorrigible sons there to be straightened out. Enrollment was less than 100 in 1879. A few years later the office of president was abolished. After the University of Texas opened, many citizens believed the A & M curriculum should be strictly limited to agricultural and mechanical courses; others thought the university should handle the educating of young Texans so that the College Station buildings could be turned into a mental institution. Former Governor Roberts complained that Aggies were being taught, at state expense, "Latin, Greek, French and all such stuff as that." They were being educated for the law and medicine, which was an outrage. Although convinced that, "Civilization begins and ends with the plow," Roberts had stated years earlier that he knew "nothing about scientific farming and cared less about it."

The embattled A & M board, trying to keep the institution alive and unmaimed, on January 1, 1890, elected Ross its president, although he could not serve until his term as governor expired in 1891. The presence of Ross at A & M worked wonders; Texans were so anxious to have their sons study under him that the 1893 enrollment reached 343 before the registrar stopped accepting applicants. Buildings were erected, the faculty and curriculum were expanded, and morale soared. The Scott Volunteers, formed in 1887, became the Ross Volunteers; a football team was organized and

This photograph of President Lawrence Sullivan Ross appears in the 1895 annual of the Agricultural and Mechanical College.

played the University of Texas for the first time in 1898. The masthead of *The Battalion*, which began publication in 1893, still carries the name of "Lawrence Sullivan Ross, Founder of Aggie Traditions, Soldier, Statesman, and Knightly Gentleman."

Ross fell ill during a Navasota River hunting trip and died January 3, 1898, but he had established public confidence in A & M. Pompeo Coppini's statue of Ross was unveiled in May, 1919, and freshmen have since demonstrated their devotion to A & M by keeping Sully well-shined. Sul Ross State Teachers College opened at Alpine in 1920.

—The Library, Texas A & M University

The condition of General Ross' statue demonstrates continued observance of the tradition of shining Sully's statue.

A & M Had More Cadets Than West Point

Texas A & M, the state's first tax-supported college, opened on October 4, 1876, at College Station; Brazos County had donated 2,416 acres for the campus. As a land grant college, A & M received an endowment of some 180,000 acres of public land, which it sold for $174,000. Vermont congressman and senator Justin Morrill had sponsored the bill providing endowments of land to the states for agricultural colleges because of the wastefulness of farmers in exhausting the vitality of soil and then moving on to repeat the process. He believed farmers should be educated in making land productive and keeping it healthy, and existing colleges confined themselves to traditional subjects, designed for prospective attorneys, preachers, and teachers; one result was that those who farmed or worked with machinery were relegated to the old ways of doing things, since institutions did not encourage research or teaching in those subjects. Morrill sought to change this.

A very important aspect of the Morrill Act was the obligation of the college to offer military training. The martial character of A & M was reflected in the *Galveston News'* reference to the first Aggies as cadets. An early rule forbade dueling, and parents sent unruly sons there in hopes that military discipline would keep them out of the penitentiary. In a 1908 dispute the students took sides against President H.H. Harrington—whose wife was Sul Ross' daughter—and began turning in their rifles.

Classes were opened and closed by bugle call. Professor David B. Cofer wrote of losing his class by such a signal:

> In the midst of my discussion of the assignment in English I heard very plainly the class recall, and thereupon my class of cadets proceeded to march out in a very orderly manner. In an half hour or so they returned....One of the cadets in Tent Row had lost some money, and so the call was sounded for assembling for inspection to get the evidence. I never learned whether the money was found or not.

President R.T. Milner, in 1910, observed:

> The Agricultural and Mechanical College of Texas presents a condition unlike that of any other educational institution in the world. Covering an area of about ten acres are stretched 243 tents in which are lodged 486 cadets. There are more students in tents than were enrolled in the college in 1906. The student body is the largest under military discipline in the world. There are 600 more cadets in this school than there are in West Point.

When war was declared the senior class of 1918 entered the officers training camp at Leon Springs; in World War I the college furnished 2,200 officers. A *New York Times* survey showed A & M first among colleges and universities in number of graduates in the services. Fifty-five Aggies were killed in action. By 1942, 6,000 Aggies had been commissioned through the ROTC program inaugurated in 1920; in World War II, 20,000 were in the armed forces, 14,000 as officers. Twenty-nine became generals, one was an admiral, and six Aggies received the Congressional Medal of Honor.

—*The Library, Texas A & M University*

Residents of an A & M dormitory engage in a general housecleaning.

Thomas Cree Planted a Tree on the High Plains

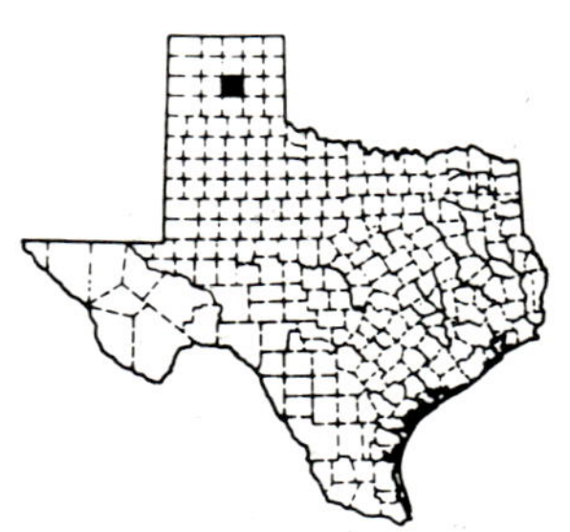

From the outset Europeans were dismayed and disturbed by the vastness of the Plains and the absence of trees. Coronado informed the Spanish king that there was not a stone, "not a bit of rising ground, not a tree, not a shrub, nor anything to go by." The flatness and the sameness of every point of the compass produced a depression, which was called "the loneliness" by some settlers and was particularly hard on women.

Thomas Cree, who settled in the Panhandle about 1886, was no stranger to the Plains. After Civil War service as a teamster he worked for the Union Pacific west of Chicago and was present at the driving of the golden spike linking the nation by rail. He helped build other railroads and farmed in his spare time. While employed by one of the companies laying track across the High Plains, Cree filed on a section of land about five miles west of Panhandle where he constructed a dugout beside a buffalo wallow. He raised hay for sale and gathered buffalo bones to be shipped east for use as fertilizer.

Everything was going well with Cree except that his wife could not accustom herself to the empty country; some trees grew in the canyons and river bottoms but there were none on the Plains. When Cree heard that the Turkey Track Ranch, thirty-five miles away, had bought some bois d'arc trees to try to grow their own fence posts, he decided to get one for her. He was ridiculed by those who believed trees could not grow on the High Plains; Cree persisted, convinced that a tree planted in Carson County could survive. In 1888 he bought a small bois d'arc from the Turkey Track and planted it in front of his dugout. A Panhandle historian wrote:

> The Johnny Appleseed of the High Plains was right when he predicted the little tree would live, and those who predicted it would not grow were also right. The little tree lived but did not grow. Each spring for the past 76 years the tiny bois d'arc has put out its green leaves.

The sight of Thomas Cree's little tree, the first planted on the High Plains, made the hard life of that country more bearable. It was a valuable landmark, and cowhands came from over the Panhandle to see the stunted bois d'arc, although it was too small to offer shelter or shade; it could only keep a person in touch with the idea of a tree.

When Cree's daughter drowned there was not a single lumber yard in the Panhandle, and her coffin had to be made from the bed of a wagon. Drouth finally drove the Crees away; in 1893 he sold his 640 acres for $50 and moved to Cheyenne, Oklahoma Territory. Seventy years afterward the tree was designated as an historical landmark by Governor John B. Connally; it prospered through cold and drouth until a state employee accidentally backed into it with a maintainer and killed it.

After being warned that it could not survive, Thomas Cree planted a bois d'arc in front of his dugout. The tree is now situated beside the Panhandle-Amarillo highway and was alive until a state maintainer backed into it.

Dodd City Staged the Great Studebaker Immolation

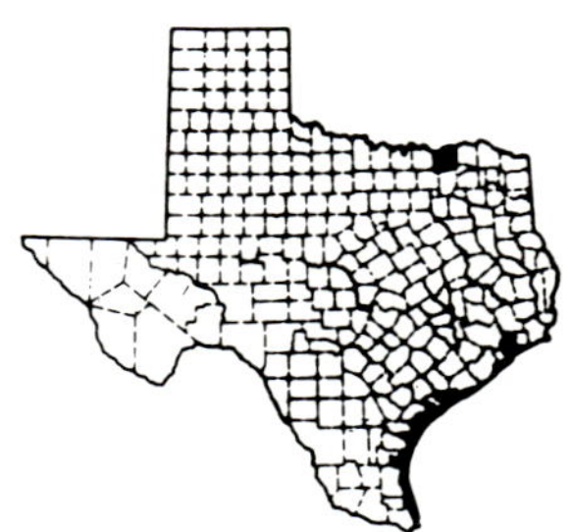

The first important event in Dodd City's history was the Rayburn family's settling nearby, and the most recent happening of significance was a visit by Boraxo's twenty mule team. By far the most memorable occurrence was an angry demonstration against certain policies of the Studebaker Company, of South Bend, Indiana. Studebaker—which was later an automobile manufacturer—was then a major wagonmaker.

After the news reached Dodd City that the Studebaker brothers had warned their employees of the dire consequences which might be expected by those who voted Democratic in the 1884 presidential election, some 200 citizens sent the following letter:

Sirs:

Since the information that you threatened to disfranchise your employees who failed to vote as you directed, we have this day made arrangements to purchase one of your wagons, "coal oil" the same and burn it in the presence of the voters of this precinct....The event will be duly advertised and published with a request that the press of the state copy the same.

We burn the "Studebaker" without knowing who will be president; we burn it in the same spirit that the tea was thrown overboard in Boston harbor in 1776; we burn it to commemorate the infamy you have heaped upon the workmen in your factory; we burn it that it may be emblazoned to Texas that you have placed a bulldozing bulletin on the walls of your factory...that we may condemn your lying cant and anathemetize your hyprocasy (sic) and that we may make your vile names odrous (sic) for all time to come, where liberty is known and freemen exist....we burn it to let our fellow countrymen of Texas know that we never desire to touch or handle any of your creations or make and that we consider the despicable coercion as treason; we burn it to consume the spokes, hubs, axles, etc., that have been made by the blood and sweat of victims whom you have reduced below the standard of manhood.

The fine people of Dodd City were as good as their word; on the main street, with appropriate ceremony, they reduced a brand new Studebaker wagon to a pile of ashes.

Outraged Dodd City citizens burned a Studebaker wagon in their main street to protest that company's requiring its employees to vote for Republican presidential electors.

Roy Bean Was the Law West of the Pecos

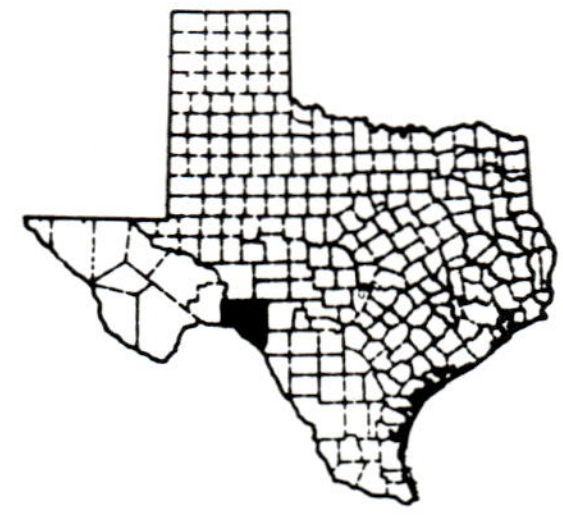

Roy Bean, born in Mason County, Kentucky, in the late 1820's, hunted for gold in California and sojourned in both Mexicos before settling in a part of San Antonio called Beanville in his honor. He hauled freight, kept a saloon, and followed other callings, always with a distinctive Bean style: as a seller of firewood his inventory came from a forest owned by a stranger, which he ravaged without permission, and as a dairyman he watered his product at a creek. (A customer allegedly received a minnow bonus in one day's milk delivery.) In the meantime the railroad had passed through San Antonio and was reaching westward to meet another line building to the east.

When someone suggested that he open a construction camp saloon along the new right of way he began to estimate how much business might result as the two gangs of workmen neared the place of joinder. The Gulf, Harrisburg and San Antonio, with an Irish crew, would meet—west of the Pecos— the Southern Pacific, whose track was being laid by hundreds of Chinese.

Bean opened a saloon in Eagle's Nest. Since the sheriff was at the Pecos County seat, Fort Stockton, 200 miles away, Rangers maintained some order, but disposition of cases after arrest remained a problem because the nearest judge was at the county seat also. For the convenience of the Rangers, in 1882, Roy Bean was appointed justice of the peace. It was the genesis of a legend, as Bean held court in his saloon in Eagle's Nest, Vinegaroon, and Langtry. The rulings and remarks of the overbearing, unlearned "Law West of the Pecos" still are quoted, although he died 73 years ago. Some familiar Roy Bean items are:

Meeting inquiries about a hurried departure from Mexico under suspicious circumstances, with the portentous explanation that, "My horse would not drink water in Mexico."

The customary conclusion of his memorable wedding ceremonies: "May God have mercy on your souls."

His contention that the granting of divorces—which was strictly beyond a justice court's jurisdiction—was proper in that it provided his only opportunity to rectify errors he might have committed in performing marriages.

His performing judicial duties—and collecting the fees—after being defeated at the polls, on the theory that "once a justice, always a justice."

Upon the discovery of a body possessed of fifty dollars and a pistol, his fining the deceased fifty dollars for carrying a concealed weapon.

Telling the governor, who charged him with exceeding his authority—which he did all the time—that the chief executive might run Austin as he wished, but that he, Bean, was the Law West of the Pecos, "by gobs, and that's my rulin."

His practice of cheating patrons of his saloon out of their change.

Barely literate, bullying, drunken old buffoon that he was, Roy Bean brought to a wild time and place a degree of order that protected life and property and permitted civilization to develop.

Judge Roy Bean, the "Law West of the Pecos," holding court at the old town of Langtry, Texas, in 1900, trying a horse thief. This building was court-house and saloon. No other peace officers in the locality at that time.

From the famous Rose Collection

—N. H. Rose Collection, Western History Collections, University of Oklahoma Library

This famous photograph, used on beer advertisements and otherwise widely circulated throughout the Southwest, shows Judge Roy Bean in front of his combination saloon and courtroom at Langtry.

Judge Roy Bean, although knowing little law, established sufficient order to permit civilization to develop in the country around Langtry.

Judge Roy Bean and his sons, Roy and Sam, and his two daughters, Zulema and Laura.

Judge Bean Hosted a Championship Fight at Langtry

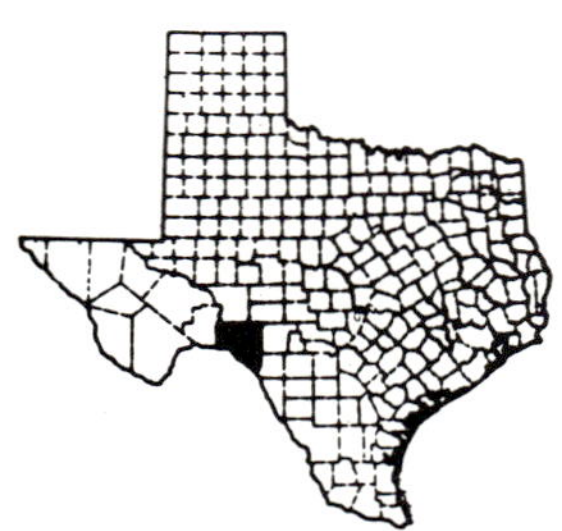

In 1895 Dan Stuart, sometime partner of Diamond Jim Brady, decided to match heavyweight champion Jim Corbett against Bob Fitzsimmons at Dallas. Texas was one of the few jurisdictions in which prize fights were legal. "Gentleman Jim" began training at San Antonio, while Fitzsimmons set up his camp at Corpus Christi. Corbett had won the crown from John L. Sullivan three years before, but by now he was more interested in a stage career than in prolonging his championship. Fitzsimmons, English-born and New Zealand-raised, was the leading contender, although he was not very large.

Dallas was getting ready for the largest crowd in its history; seating for 53,000 was under construction at the fair grounds, and cafe and hotel proprietors were preparing to serve the visitors. As the excitement mounted, critics of boxing began to exert pressure on the governor; the sport was brutal and a favorite of gamblers, they said. Governor Charles Culberson, giving in to their strident protests, called a special session of the legislature to prohibit prize fights. After this bit of idiocy was accomplished the match was moved to Hot Springs, frightening the Arkansas governor, who would not permit it to be held there. The fight fell through.

In late 1895, Corbett retired and declared Peter Maher to be the heavyweight champion, something he had no right to do. Maher, born in Ireland, had been knocked out by Fitzsimmons three years earlier, but now Stuart made a new match between Maher and Fitzsimmons the grand finale of a Fight Carnival to be staged "in or near El Paso," in spite of Governor Culberson's warnings. Stuart apparently thought El Paso—600 miles from Austin—was too remote for the state to really care. Also he could move into Mexico, Arizona, or New Mexico if Texas acted to stop the bout. Since the fight was to be filmed, and the movie income was substantial, neither the site nor the size of the crowd was really important. Maher began training at Las Cruces, New Mexico, and Bob Fitzsimmons, accompanied by his pet lion, Nero, opened his camp at Juárez.

The politicians were willing to go to incredible lengths in appeasing the anti-prizefight faction. Adjutant General Mabry took the Rangers to El Paso, which was a break for Texas bad men. With almost the entire force several hundred miles away, the Rangers did not exist for the rest of the state. Still selling tickets for the fight on February 15, 1896, Stuart brought in gunman Bat Masterson to insure that the match could be held.

Fight fans poured into El Paso from all over the country and waited for Stuart to announce where the event would occur. While building materials for the ring and bleachers—and the moving picture equipment—remained on railroad cars, the Rangers followed Fitzsimmons everywhere, and deputy U.S. marshals shadowed Maher. February 15 came and went without any statement by Stuart. The Rangers prevented any attempt to hold the fight in El Paso, officials of the Territory of New Mexico had their border guarded, and Mexican troops would not allow Stuart to bring his fighters into Chihuahua. Furthermore the Arizona governor announced that he was holding the militia in readiness should the fight head that way.

Maher-Fitzsimmons fight was promoted by Judge Roy Bean,"Law West of the Pecos," on an island in Rio Grande river, near Langtry,Texas,1896. Fitzsimmons won, in first round.

The canvas curtain was supposed to shield from view the Fitzsimmons-Maher fight at Langtry, Texas, but most of the non-paying spectators were seated on the bluff from which this photograph was taken.

The Tuscon *Citizen* commented:

> Of all the continental tomfoolery the territory of Arizona has ever been guilty of the worst is sending the Arizona Militia to chase jack rabbits up and down the San Simon Valley....The idea of ordering out three or four companies of militia to stop a couple of windy pugs from pummelling one another is a ridiculous farce. If the brutes cross the line, let the sheriff of the county arrest them, or better yet, let them fight if they want to. They will not hurt one another and if they do what difference does it make to anyone in Arizona?

Then Stuart announced that spectators were to board an eastbound train for an undisclosed destination on the evening of February 20. On the following day the fans and Rangers got off at Langtry, Judge Roy Bean's town, some 400 miles southeast of El Paso on the Río Grande. They found that Bean had provided a pontoon footbridge across the river to Coahuila, where a ring surrounded by a canvas screen had been built on a sand flat. The 200 spectators would stand during the altercation, which was outside Ranger jurisdiction and at a place too remote to be reached in season by Mexican troops. Unfortunately for Stuart, observers—including all the Rangers—could sit on the bluffs on the Texas side of the river and watch the boxers without paying admission.

About 4:30 the fight began. Maher weighed less than 200 pounds; even so he had a 30-pound advantage over Fitzsimmons. The challenger had asked for part of the movie revenues, and one writer assumed that Stuart's refusal was the reason Fitzsimmons made such quick work of Maher. A minute and a half into the first round Fitzsimmons knocked out Maher and became the new heavyweight champion of the world. One sportsman, who had come all the way from New York and spent several days waiting around El Paso, turned around to get a light for his cigar, and when he looked back to the ring Maher was already unconscious. Then someone shouted a warning that the Río Grande was rising, so the fans hurried back across the bridge to drink more of the beer Judge Bean was selling at highly inflated prices. Within the hour fighters, spectators, and Rangers had departed by train for El Paso. The event that had precipitated congressional action and a special session of the Texas legislature, the passage of new laws for Texas and the territories, the massing of troops by a foreign nation and the territories of New Mexico and Arizona, and the relinquishment of Ranger protection for most of Texas, had passed into history in less than two minutes with the only damage being that done to Pete Maher's head and the taxpayers' pocketbooks.

In the next year, "Gentleman Jim" Corbett, having come out of retirement, Fitzsimmons rendered him senseless at Carson City, Nevada.

Fans arriving at Langtry from El Paso for the Fitzsimmons-Maher fight used this bridge to get to the ring that had been erected across the Río Grande.

Group of Texas Rangers from the four Battalions, headed by Adjutant-General Mabry, detailed to prevent the Maher-Fitzsimmons prize fight taking place in Texas, in 1896. The fight took place in Mexico, opposite Langtry, Texas, (Roy Bean's town) while the rangers looked on from the American side. No.1--Adjutant-General W.H.Mabry; 2-Captain John R. Hughes; 3-Captain J.A.Brooks; 4-Captain W.J.McDonald; 5-Captain J.H.Rogers; 6--Creed Taylor; 7-John Hess; 8-Bob Chew; 9--Throckmorton; 10--J.H.Evetts; 11--George Horton; 12--Billy McCauley; 13-Lee Queen; 14-Jim(Wooly)Bell; 15-Ed.Flint; 16-James Fulgham; 17-Ed.Donley; 18-Sgt.W. J. L. Sullivan; 19-Jack Harwell; 20-Bob McClure; 21-Ed.Conley; 22-Andy Ferguson; 23-W.M.Burwell; 24-John Moore; 25-C.F.Heirs; 26-C.L.(Kid) Rogers; 27-T.T.Cook; 28-Doc Neal; 29-Edgar Neil; 30-Ed.Bryant; 31-Doctor Lozier; 32-George Tucker.

—Western History Collections, University of Oklahoma Library

Most of the Rangers were sent to El Paso to keep Fitzsimmons and Maher from fighting for the Heavyweight Championship in Texas.

—*Western History Collections, University of Oklahoma Library*

Bat Masterson, a famous gunman and participant in the Second Battle of Adobe Walls, was hired to make sure that the Fitzsimmons-Maher fight could be held.

Brann Was Killed on a Waco Street

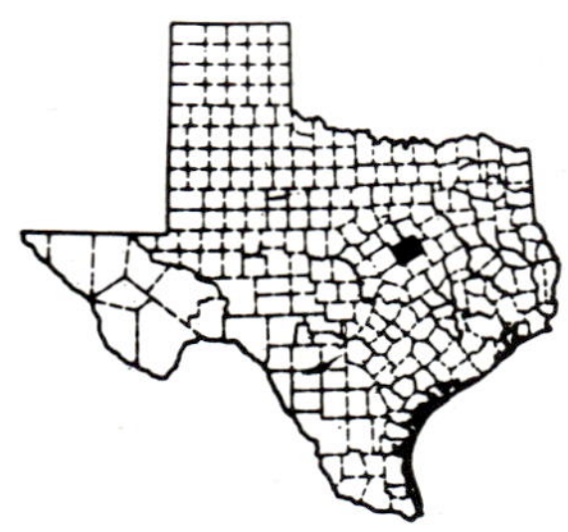

On April Fool's Day, 1898, on a Waco street, William Cowper Brann was shot in the back "right where the suspenders crossed." He was known all over the country because of his magazine, *The Iconoclast*, whose circulation was five times Waco's population of 25,000. The Illinois-born son of a Presbyterian minister, Brann was raised by foster parents after his mother's death. He went to work young; having been everything from semi-professional baseball pitcher to I.G.N. Railway brakeman, in 1883 he became a *St. Louis Globe-Democrat* reporter. He moved on to the *Galveston Evening Tribune*, the *Galveston News*, and the *Houston Post*, where he was the chief editorial writer.

After his thirteen-year-old daughter killed herself, in the summer of 1890, Brann began publishing *The Austin Iconoclast*, which would provide a forum for his strong opinions. Public response was slight, and Brann returned to the *St. Louis Globe-Democrat*, leaving a manager to run the *Iconoclast*. Brann sold the *Iconoclast* to William Sidney Porter, who would later write as O. Henry.

Brann left the *Express* after a disagreement and barely made a living until he joined the *Waco Daily News* in late 1894. Waco, the "Athens of Texas" because of Baylor University and other educational institutions, was also celebrated for frontier violence, saloons, and one of the nation's two legal red light districts. (Omaha, Nebraska, maintained the other.) Waco had plenty of churches, and Baptists were particularly strong.

After a few months Brann revived *The Iconoclast*, which sold for a dime and was sixteen, two-columned pages of strong, unorthodox religious and political opinion. The attention it attracted increased as attacks upon the Waco establishment intensified. The influential Baptist churches, Baylor University and its president, the Reverend Rufus Burleson, received much unfavorable comment. In the summer of 1895 the brother of Burleson's son-in-law was indicted for the rape of a sixteen-year-old Brazilian girl who lived in the Burleson home. After Dr. Burleson assailed her character, telling a reporter "I think the idea of rape in this case is simply preposterous," Brann mounted a vicious attack on Baylor and the Baptists.

Racist and often mistaken, Brann was always entertaining, particularly when examining the actions and motives of preachers, reformers, and politicians; their efforts against boxing was perfect fodder for him. He claimed the movement exhausted the Fool-killer; the furor over the Fitzsimmons fights revealed that there were simply too many fools. Brann was upset:

> ...to see a lot of plotting politicians and half-baked preachers tearing around like a hen on a hot griddle, or a skye-terrier with a clothes-pin anchored to his tail, simply because a couple of professional pugs want to pound each other with feather pillows for a fat purse. I cannot see, to save me, where their kick comes in. Suppose the pugilists do maim each other: who will mourn? Not the ministers; for, to judge by their utterances, they would gladly see the whole gang under the grass. If they kill each other, who will weep? Not the politicians—they have trouble of their own. "But the public will be corrupted," I am told. The public appears amply able to take care of itself—it has put more than a thousand preachers in the penitentiary. The

William Cowper Brann's Waco journal of opinion, *The Iconoclast*, attracted a world-wide readership. Its circulation was four times the population of Waco.

modern politicians "guarding public morals" are like setting the wolf to watch the lamb....There's Culberson, for instance—"our heroic young Christian governor"—what? Imagine Son Charles guarding anything—except...a stack of poker chips! Think of that crap-shooting, chippy-chasing legislature—with its pockets full of complimentary passes—shielding Texas from pugilistic contamination....

I am assured by the ministers that..."none but the roughs and rowdies gather at the ringside." How can a prizefight, however brutal, "corrupt" cattle of that kind? How can you...debase those already debauched? If El Paso is willing to be made the rendezvous of all the roughs and rowdies, should not all the rest of Christendom rejoice over the "good riddance of bad rubbish?"

To prevent this awful catastrophe Culberson called a special session of the legislature and massed the Rangers on the Rio Grande. To prevent it Cleveland deprived himself of a duck hunt and remained reasonably sober an entire day. Public sentiment is supposed to be "agin" prize-fights; ergo, the politians oppose it...."You can't sometimes most always tell" about this thing we call public sentiment. If Corbett and Fitzsimmons were to fight in Dallas today—without admission fee—Waco, the religious hub of the world, would be depopulated. Half the preachers of Texas would go early to secure front seats.

Neither the sporty governor of Texas nor the immaculate ass who officiates as chief magistrate of New Mexico ever thought of interfering with prize-fighting until a match was made between two men of international reputation and the politicians thereby accorded an opportunity to make a grandstand demonstration.

Prospering, Brann rented offices in the Provident Building and hired employees to manage the journal's business. The fact that the *Iconoclast* had subscribers all over the world made its attacks harder for victims to bear. After statements like, "As Baylor cannot very well become worse it must of necessity become better," in October, 1897, angry students took Brann, at gunpoint, to the Baylor campus. While his arms were tied a lynch mob beat him about the head. Some professors intervened, but his captors forced Brann to sign an admission that he had lied and promise to leave Waco by sundown.

A few days later Judge John Scarbrough caned Brann while his son, George, a Baylor student, held a gun on him and another young man belabored him with a horsewhip. Brann managed to escape with a broken arm. In a dispute growing out of the *Iconoclast's* troubles, Judge G.B. Gerald, a Brann supporter, shot and killed W.A. Harris and his brother, editor J.W. Harris of the *Waco Times-Herald*.

Brann kept up his attacks and dared his enemies to respond. Mentioning rumors then current that Dallas would pay Baylor $50,000 to move there, he promised $1,000 if Baylor would leave Waco and another $1,000 if the new site were as distant as Honolulu. When threats against him increased, Brann decided to deliver some lectures away from Waco.

On the day before his first speaking engagement he was walking along 4th Street with William Ward when Tom Davis came out of an office and shot Brann in the back. Brann then shot Davis, and Ward was wounded in the hand as he grabbed Davis' pistol. Both Brann and Davis kept firing. After Brann was arrested and taken to the police station, two blocks away, the officers found that he had been hit three times. He died at his home the next morning, a few hours ahead of Davis, who had been shot four times. Davis' motives were never known. His daughter attended Baylor, which may or may not have been relevant. There is no evidence that he had ever met Brann.

Brann's tombstone in Waco's Oakwood Cemetery bears his image, which has been damaged by vandals' pistol shots.

William C. Brann was buried in Waco's Oakwood Cemetery. Vandals have shot at the headstone, as the chipped places at Brann's temple indicate.

Wes Hardin Died in an El Paso Saloon

John Wesley Hardin, born in Bonham, Fannin County, on May 26, 1853, to the Reverend James Gipson Hardin and Mary Elizabeth Dixon Hardin, killed his first man when he was fifteen and had 26 notches on his gun before his nineteenth birthday. Hardin was a gunfighter; he did not kill for hire or in support of some other criminal activity; instead his killing grew out of a contentiousness, a belligerence, a compulsion to test himself and others which regularly put him in a position of defending his life or vindicating what he considered to be his honor.

Hardin's first serious trouble occurred when he was about twelve; a schoolmaster who pulled a knife was stabbed twice for his trouble. Three years later Hardin and another were matched to wrestle a black man named Maze, who had a formidable local reputation because of his size and strength. As the boys bested him, the fifteen-year-old Hardin accidentally scratched his face. Maze swore revenge, and meeting Hardin on a country road, tried to pull him off his horse. Hardin shot him twice. After Maze's death, the Reverend Hardin, fearful that the Unionists and carpetbaggers would not permit a fair trial, sent his son away; this was the beginning of years of violence as Wes Hardin evaded capture. Because of the unpopularity of the federal army of occupation and hatred of Republican governor Davis' state police, Hardin was able to live rather openly with kinsmen.

When a Comanche County mob was frustrated in its efforts to catch Wes Hardin, it hanged his older brother—respected local attorney Joe Hardin—and two of his Dixon cousins, on a live oak tree on Comanche's courthouse square.

Hardin was living in Florida as J.H. Swain when the Texas legislature offered $4,000 for his capture; it was the largest such reward ever posted by the state. Ranger John Armstrong and Dallas detective Jack Dawson captured Hardin a few miles from Polland, Alabama, where Mrs. Hardin had relatives. They brought him back to Texas to stand trial for the shooting of Charles Webb, a Brown County deputy sheriff who—out of his jurisdiction—was killed in Comanche by Hardin in a fair fight. Pending trial Hardin was kept in the Travis County jail to frustrate lynch mobs. He was taken to Comanche, cuffed and shackled, by 21 rangers, a sheriff, and five deputies. Fifty Comanche county citizens were deputized to help guard him from the crowd that had threatened to hang him. But the most effective restraint was the Rangers' warning that in the event of trouble Hardin would be given two guns and turned loose.

At the trial Hardin had no witnesses and was not permitted to testify in his own behalf. Prosecution witnesses said Webb fired first, which would have justified an acquittal on the ground of self-defense, but the jury convicted him of second-degree murder. He began serving a 25-year term at Huntsville in October, 1878. After unsuccessful escape attempts, solitary confinement, floggings, and other punishment, Hardin settled down. He was superintendent of the prison Sunday school, read constantly, and began to study law. Although Hardin killed more than 40 men his only trial, other than the one at Comanche, was on a Cuero manslaughter indictment. His wife, Jane, supported herself and their three children, Molly, John, Jr., and Jane; she

John Wesley Hardin, the worst of the badmen, killed about 40 men and served time for the murder of a Brown County deputy sheriff. After he was pardoned he practiced law.

died in 1892 at the age of 36.

On February 17, 1897, Hardin was released from prison, his sentence having been reduced by the good time he had served. Governor Jim Hogg granted him a full pardon. At Gonzales Hardin was admitted to the practice of law. He moved to Junction and married Callie Lewis, who was much younger than he was; they never lived together. Hardin was in Kerrville working on his autobiography when Jim Miller's friends got him to help prosecute G.A. Frazier for shooting Miller. While the case was pending at Pecos, he worked on his book in El Paso, the last outpost of the Texas bad men, who respected and feared Hardin; a few hoped to enhance their reputations by killing him. After some trouble with policeman John Selman, Jr., on August 19, 1895, Hardin was playing dice at the bar in the Acme Saloon when Constable John Selman, Sr., shot him in the back.

El Paso was still a rough frontier town. W.W. Mills wrote:

> The next day after the notorious ex-convict and desperado, Wesley Harden [sic] was killed on San Antonio street by a worse man than himself, who was a constable or something, people, though not sorry at Harden's taking off, were shocked at the manner of it, but feared to condemn the act, because no one knew who would be the next victim.

—*Western History Collections, University of Oklahoma Library*

Instead of extraditing John Wesley Hardin from Alabama, the Texas governor simply sent Ranger John Armstrong and a companion to kidnap Hardin.

A Storm Destroyed Galveston

On September 1, 1900, Galveston was a leading Texas city. It had 37,000 residents, was a commercial center, and was perhaps the nation's leading shipper of cotton. But Galveston Island's highest point was just 15 feet above sea level and the best elevation in town, on Broadway, was less than 9 feet above the water. One week later a storm that had originated 5,000 miles away turned Galveston into a ruined, stinking, sodden mass of dead people, animals, homes, and hopes.

On September 4, the Weather Bureau in Washington had notified Galveston by telegraph that the storm was following a northwestward course past Cuba. By Friday morning, September 7, it was approaching the Louisiana coast, and warnings were extended to Galveston; while the storm center was still 200 miles away, the tide had risen enough to cause flooding in Galveston by four o'clock Saturday morning, September 8. The water rose all morning and when the last train arrived from Houston, at 11 a.m., the tracks across the bay were only two feet above water. A heavy rain was falling and a 30-mile-an-hour wind was blowing.

By noon the wind, gusting up to 75 miles an hour, was knocking out window panes in downtown Galveston; falling glass and flying slate shingles injured and killed several people. The water was rising at the rate of 15 inches an hour. The railroad tracks were under water and the telephone and telegraph lines to the mainland were down before four o'clock. Water from the bay had met that from the Gulf and stood a foot deep on Galveston's highest point. Debris swept along by the current knocked people down and carried them away. Then the entire island was submerged, and wreckage sped from bay to Gulf and back, battering those buildings which remained standing. The wind ranged from 85 to 100 miles an hour; and residents were washed out to sea clinging to their wrecked homes. At eight p.m. the high water mark was reached, measuring 10½ feet at Union Station and almost 16 feet at other points.

The storm center passed Galveston before ten o'clock that night, and the water fell quickly, exposing great heaps of broken walls and roofs that had been buildings and bodies of thousands of humans and animals and trees. Ships torn loose from anchorage had been thrown against each other and beached. No streets were visible; passage was across shattered buildings and past the dead; an inch of thick mud covered everything.

When looting began, on Sunday, temporary officers were appointed and ordered to shoot anyone caught stealing. The cemeteries were overlaid by mud and there were not enough men to dig the necessary graves, so on Monday firemen and others began loading bodies on barges for burial at sea; men refusing to volunteer were forced to work at gunpoint, and when the task became unbearable a priest gave them whiskey. By nightfall some 700 bodies were loaded, towed into the Gulf, and dumped. By morning, Tuesday, many had washed ashore. To prevent the disease that would surely follow, the workers began burning bodies. Nearly 1/3 of the residential area was gone; the mayor believed 5,000 people had died and could only guess how many were homeless and destitute. Many years later the number of deaths still could not be determined with any certainty. Estimates were 4,000 to 12,000, but probably the most

Typical of conditions in Galveston following the storm was the intersection of 21st and Avenue O on September 9, 1900.

reliable was computed by editors of the 1901 City Directory, 6,000 dead.

Martial law was declared on September 13, as soldiers, police and firemen tried to keep sightseers out. A report to Governor Sayers read:

> The situation beggars description. I am convinced that the city is practically wrecked for all time to come. Fully 75 per cent of the business of the town is irreparably wrecked, and the same per cent of damage is to be found in the residence district. Along the wharf great ocean steamers have bodily bumped themselves on the big piers and lie there, great masses of iron and wood...the great warehouses along the waterfront are smashed in on one side, unroofed and gutted throughout their length, their contents either piled in heaps on the wharves or along the streets. Small tugs and sailboats have jammed themselves half into the buildings, where they were landed by the incoming waves and left by receding waters.
>
> Great piles of human bodies, dead animals, rotting vegetation, household furniture, and fragments of houses are piled in confused heaps right in the main streets of the city. Along the gulf front human bodies are floating around like cordwood. Intermingled with them are to be found the carcasses of horses, chickens, dogs, and rotting vegetable matter.

Some 2,500 men were engaged in searching residential areas for the dead while 5,000 others were clearing and rebuilding the wharves. Clara Barton, of the American Red Cross, came to Galveston and issued a plea for material sufficient to build 8,000 houses. So effective were efforts at relief and rehabilitation that less than two months later—on November 1, 1900—39 freighters were working cargo at Galveston's docks.

Clara Barton took Red Cross Volunteers to Galveston to assist in caring for survivors of the storm. She was 78 at the time, and this was the last occasion in which she actively participated in disaster relief work.

Galvestonians, trying to avoid another catastrophe such as that of September, 1900, appointed a board which recommended building a seawall and raising the grade of the island.

—*Rosenberg Library*

After completion of the seawall the next step was to elevate the land so water would drain off. This delivery wagon is halted by a portion of roadway which has been raised.

The Galvestonians Built a Seawall

A week after the September, 1900, storm Colonel R.G. Love, the *Galveston Daily News* manager, wired this assessment—which proved to be an understatement—to the Associated Press in New York:

> The summary of conditions prevailing at Galveston is more than human intellect can master. Briefly stated the damage to property is anywhere between $15,000,000 and $20,000,000. The loss of life cannot be computed. No list could be kept, and all is simple guess work. Those thrown out to sea and buried in the ground will reach the horrible total of at least 3,000 souls. My estimate of the loss on the island of Galveston is between 4,000 and 5,000 deaths. I do not make this statement in fright or excitement. The whole story will never be told.
>
> The necessities of those living are total. Not a single individual escaped property loss. The property on the island is wrecked, fully one half totally swept out of existence altogether....The help must be immediate.

But in spite of 6,000 deaths and 3,600 ruined homes the *News* also predicted that "inside of two years there will exist upon the island of Galveston a city three times greater than the one which has just been partially destroyed."

After the wreckage was cleaned up and rebuilding had begun some Galvestonians wondered if another such catastrophe could be prevented. In the early days fifteen-foot sand dunes protected the island's interior from the Gulf, but these handy sources of fill dirt had been removed to facilitate access to the beach; by 1900 Galveston was unprotected.

The committee appointed to find a solution was headed by the retired chief of army engineers, Brigadier General H.M. Robert, author of *Robert's Rules of Order*. In January, 1902, the Robert board suggested building a concrete wall whose top would be 17 feet above mean low tide; since the storm's highest water had been less than 16 feet, that elevation was sure to be adequate. To support the wall and provide drainage the level of the city was to be raised, sloped from seawall to bay at one foot per 1,500 feet of distance. Immediately behind the wall would be an embankment accomodating a roadway. The solid concrete seawall, set on pilings driven to a depth of 44 feet, would be 16 feet thick at the base and 5 feet in thickness at the top. The face would have a concave curve to break the force of the waves and direct them upward. The entire lower portion of the wall would be protected by a riprap of granite boulders three feet deep and 27 feet wide. The county agreed to build the wall, and the city would be responsible for the grade work.

This first seawall, about three miles long, was begun in October, 1902, and finished in July, 1904, at a cost of $1,581,673.30. Enthusiastic citizens approved the issuance of county bonds by a vote of 3,084 to 21, and when bond buyers were not interested, Galvestonians, from laborers to bankers, bought all but $250,000 of the $1.5 million issue. While the first construction was in progress the United States began building the 4,935-foot seawall in front of Fort Crockett between 37th and 53rd streets. The seawall's worth was proved in 1915 when a tropical cyclone as bad as the 1900 storm

St. Patrick's Church, the largest Galveston building to be raised, continued to be used for mass while suspended five feet in the air by jacks.

caused only 12 deaths and property damage 80% less than that of the earlier disaster. Improvements were made in the seawall as a result of lessons learned in 1915 and later. By the time Hurricane Carla struck in 1961—on the anniversary of the 1900 storm—the seawall was 7.29 miles long; it has since been lengthened to about 10 miles.

The raising of Galveston's grade—a more spectacular achievement than the seawall— was begun in 1903 and supervised by a board appointed by Governor Lanham. Financing the project was difficult because most bond buyers believed Galveston could never recover financially. Only two bidders sought the grade-raising job because of uncertainty that it could be done. The $6 million cost was borne by the city; the state helped by turning over some $4 million of tax revenues. Elevation of the grade involved raising more than 2,500 homes and the water and gas lines and other utilities serving them. Churches, streets, sidewalks, and railroad tracks all had to be adjusted to the new level.

A 2.5-mile canal, 200 feet wide and 20 feet deep, was dug behind the seawall to accomodate the dredges; the houses were moved to temporary locations and then brought back after the work was completed and the canal filled in. Four German-built dredges were used; the largest, the *Leviathan*, could haul 1,500 yards of fill. They took sand from the bottom of the bay, came up the canal, and discharged the fill material onto the areas to be raised; the water drained into the canal as the sand dried. In some parts of town a canal was not needed, and sandy water was simply pumped to donee areas, some of them 19,000 feet from the source. The first project was completed, and the canal was filled in 1910. By 1931 the various contractors had moved more than 30 million cubic yards of fill into Galveston.

In spring, 1907, the large structures such as Grace Episcopal Church were raised. St. Patrick's Catholic Church—at 3,000 tons the largest—was elevated five feet "without loss of a single brick and without any interruption of its use," according to the *Galveston News*, which also noted that, "People continued to live in their elevated houses while the mucky sand from the bottom of the bay was pumped under them. Even flower gardens were saved by transplanting the plants to boxes and then replanting them when the surface of the ground had been raised." In the meantime engineering and scientific journals were informing the world about the miracle in progress at Galveston.

St. Patrick's Church, Galveston, as it appears today.

Albert Lasker Fathered Modern Advertising

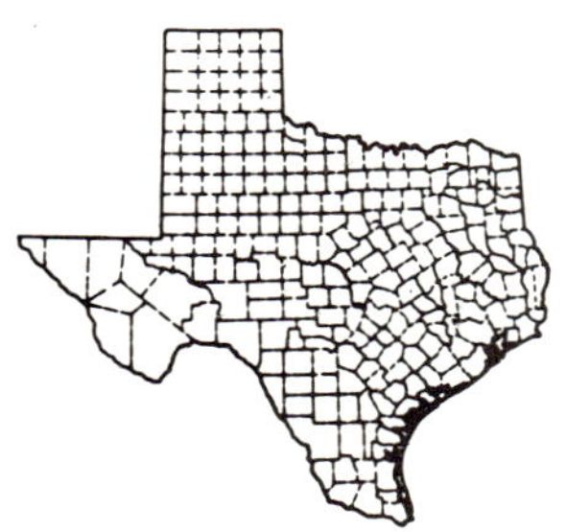

Morris Lasker, a German Jew, settled in Texas before the Civil War and was a leading Galveston businessman in 1880 when his son, Albert, was born. Albert Davis Lasker built the world's largest advertising agency, introduced dozens of products which became institutions, and provided early opportunities for such unknown performers as Bing Crosby and Bob Hope. At the age of twelve Lasker wrote and published the *Galveston Free Press*, a four-page weekly which earned a regular profit in its one year. At thirteen he was a part-time *Galveston Morning News* reporter, and upon graduating from Ball High School in 1896 he became a regular employee. R.B. Hawley hired the sixteen-year-old to write speeches and help in his congressional campaign and became the first Republican elected from the old Confederacy since the close of Reconstruction.

In 1897 Lasker launched the boxing career of young Jack Johnson, a Galveston boy who would become the first black heavyweight champion, and in the next year he went to work for Lord and Thomas, a Chicago advertising agency, for $10 a week; although it was one of the world's three largest agencies, annual billings were less than a million dollars. Advertising men then limited their services to obtaining newspaper space for clients. Not a single agency had a copy writer; creative advertising was really the domain of the patent medicine companies.

In the next 44 years Lasker bought Lord and Thomas. John Gunther said:

> He made $45,000,000 by sheer brain power. His fortune did not come from...the mass production and sale of some such commodity as automobiles, nor through speculation, nor by the lucky ownership of property bearing oil or some similar natural resource. He made the bulk of his fortune by communicating abstractions—by ideas.

Businesses were not convinced of the value of advertising at the turn of the century; Wrigley's initial budget was $32.00 and that of the Borden Company was $513.75. Lord and Thomas was the first agency to hire copy writers. Representing Sunkist Growers, Lasker raised orange consumption tremendously. Lord and Thomas took the unknown Palmolive, which was distinguished only by its green color in 1911, and made it the nation's best selling hand soap; it successfully promoted Van Camp's pork and beans when 94% of American women baked their own. When, in 1913, the agency changed the names of Quaker Oats' Wheat Berries and Puffed Berries to Puffed Rice and Puffed Wheat—and claimed they were "shot from guns"—demand soared.

With chewing gum manufacturer William Wrigley and meat packer J. Ogden Armour, Lasker owned the Chicago Cubs. He not only introduced Kleenex and Frigidaire and sold Studebaker automobiles, but he turned Lucky Strike into a top brand and persuaded women to smoke; his later efforts put the American Cancer Society on a solid footing for the first time. Pioneering radio advertising, he hired Freeman Gosden and Charles Correll to broadcast "Amos n' Andy" and put Bob Hope on the radio for Pepsodent. With "The Story of Mary Marlin," Lord and Thomas invented the soap opera; its other shows included "Your Hit Parade," "Information Please," "Mr. District Attorney," and "Lum and Abner."

Galveston's Albert Lasker promoted the match between Jack Johnson and Joe Choynski
and founded modern advertising.

Jack Johnson Was the First Black Heavyweight Champion

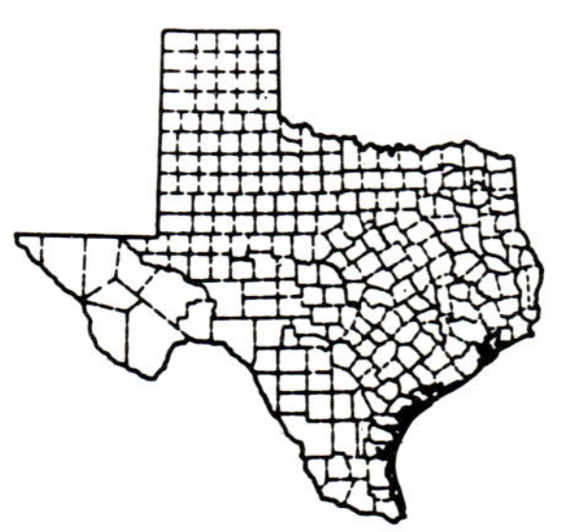

John Arthur Johnson, born in Galveston on March 31, 1878, left school after the fifth grade and held a multitude of jobs, including custodian at a gymnasium. There he decided he wanted to become a fighter. When a carnival owner offered five dollars to anyone who could stay four rounds with his boxer, Johnson won. He probably fought professionally for the first time in a match arranged by Albert Lasker with Joe Choynski, a Polish Jew, at Galveston. Lasker had offered Choynski $500 to fight the "Dixie Champ", but when Choynski reached Galveston the "Dixie Champ" fled. The seventeen-year-old Lasker, afraid of having to make refunds on the tickets he had sold, while still having to pay Choynski, offered Jack Johnson $25 to take the place of the "Dixie Champ." Johnson lost, and both boxers were arrested for violating the statute forbidding prize fights. During the two or three weeks they spent in the Galveston jail, Choynski taught Johnson the things he needed to know to become a professional boxer. (Johnson's autobiography says the Choynski fight took place at least as late as 1901, after he had fought professionally several times.)

In the next few years Johnson's earnings and reputation as a boxer grew. He bought his first car in 1904, beginning a career as a notoriously reckless driver; he would have many minor accidents and accumulate hundreds of tickets before his death in a car wreck 42 years later. Johnson was a contender, but the heavyweight crown was firmly held by James J. Jeffries, who had won the title from Bob Fitzsimmons in 1899. Jeffries, undefeated, in 1905, staged a match in which Marvin Hart beat Jack Root. He then resigned and gave the heavyweight championship to Hart, something Jeffries had no right to do.

Canadian Noah Brusso, who boxed under the name of Tommy Burns, defeated Hart in November, 1906. Burns was only five feet seven inches tall and weighed 180, but he defended the title successfully several times while avoiding the six foot two inch, 200-pound Johnson. In the meantime Johnson defeated former champion Bob Fitzsimmons and Sam Langford. When John L. Sullivan—"the Great John L."—claimed his fighter, Kid Cutler, could whip Johnson, he was quickly scheduled, and Johnson knocked him out with one punch. On the day after Christmas, 1908, at Sidney, Australia, Jack Johnson defeated Tommy Burns to become the first black heavyweight champion.

Although Johnson defeated Stanley Ketchel and other worthy contenders—including movie actor and Academy Award winner Victor McLaghlen—many fight fans refused to recognize his title. Johnson's second wife was a white woman—as also would be his third and fourth wives—which antagonized his critics; they began wishing for someone to defeat him, to recover the title. Seeking a "white hope" to humble Johnson it was only natural that they try to get Jeffries to come out of retirement and reclaim the heavyweight crown. Jeffries was too old, and he weighed more than 300 pounds, but he yielded to the cajolery of the racists. His preparations for the fight were supervised by former champion, "Gentleman Jim" Corbett. He trained hard.

—*Library of Congress*

Jack Johnson successfully defended his heavyweight title against Jim Flynn.

The Jeffries fight, promoted by George Lewis Rickard, a former Texas peace officer, was to be held in San Francisco, but reform groups forced its removal to Reno. Nevada had only 40,000 residents and was the sole American jurisdiction in which prize fighting was legal; promoters in other states evaded the law—not always successfully—by advertising their matches as exhibitions. Before 15,000 people, including newspaper correspondents Jack London, Rex Beach, and John L. Sullivan on July 4, 1900, Johnson met Jeffries. "Tex" Rickard required the spectators to give up their pistols before entering the stadium. The betting was 10 to 6 in Jeffries' favor, the result of wishful thinking; Jeffries was simply too old. Beneath a hot sun Johnson administered a terrible beating and knocked out the former champion in the fifteenth round. Johnson's earnings for this match exceeded $100,000—more than any athlete or entertainer had ever received for a single performance. The *Galveston Daily News* reported that, "John Arthur Johnson, tonight is the undisputed champion of the world."

He opened the Cafe de Champion in Chicago in 1911, the year the first "White Hope Tourney" was held to find someone able to vanquish Johnson. His enemies criticized him because of troubles at his cafe and his gambling, frequent arrests for speeding, his flamboyance—and because of their prejudice. He was indicted, tried, and convicted of violating the Mann Act, and he fled the country rather than serve the one year sentence imposed by the court.

Johnson reached Europe in July, 1913. He was not welcome in England, and when he defeated Frank Moran in France the fight proceeds were impounded and Johnson was never paid. The outbreak of World War I in the following year made it difficult to arrange matches or to pursue the theatrical career he was attempting. Then he was contacted in behalf of the latest white hope, the six foot, six inch, 250-pound Jess Willard. Again the site was a problem; he could not return to the United States without being arrested, and the European nations were too much preoccupied with the war. Juárez, Mexico, would have served the purpose, but President Carranza did not want Johnson to come there. So at Havana, Cuba, on April 5, 1915, in an atmosphere and amid surroundings reminiscent of Reno and the Jeffries match, the fight took place. But now Johnson, at 37, was too old and out of condition; he had trained only briefly and occasionally. Willard, in good shape, was going strong long after Johnson was gasping for breath in the 103 degree heat. Willard knocked him out in the 26th round.

Jack Johnson never made a serious attempt to recover his title. He fought bulls in Spain and Mexico and made stage appearances. He returned to the United States in 1920, surrendered to the authorities, and served his prison sentence. Afterward he made inspirational talks, staged boxing exhibitions, and was a Coney Island sideshow attraction. While returning to New York from performing in the south he wrecked his Lincoln near Franklinton, North Carolina, and died in a Raleigh hospital on June 10, 1946.

Joe Louis—the great Brown Bomber—was the champion then, and the minister at Johnson's funeral noted, "If we hadn't had a Jack then, we wouldn't have a Joe now." Earlier Nat Fleischer, the publisher of *Ring* magazine had called Jack Johnson "the greatest heavyweight who ever lived."

—U. S. Information Agency, *National Archives*

Heavyweight champion Jack Johnson, convicted of a Mann Act violation, fled to Europe.
He is shown here in Paris.

"Tex" Rickard Matched Johnson Against the Great White Hope

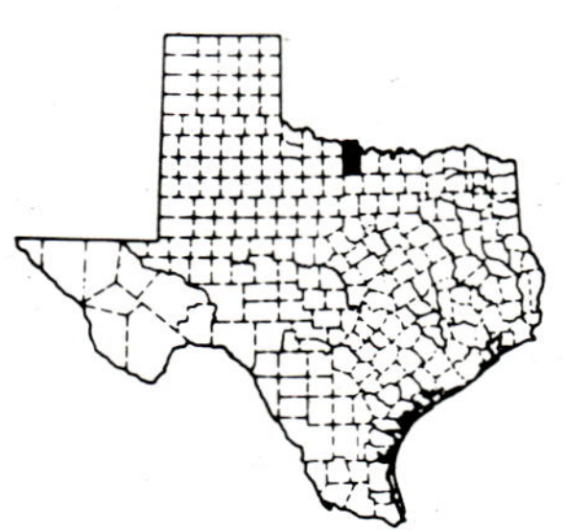

George Lewis Rickard was born in Clay County, Missouri, January 2, 1871, on a farm adjoining that of Jesse James' mother. His family moved to Clay County, Texas, where his father died in 1882 and he quit school in the third grade; as an eleven-year-old, Rickard was a wrangler and a cowboy in the last days of trail driving. In 1894 he married and was elected Henrietta City Marshal, but after his wife and baby died, in 1895, he headed for Alaska's gold fields.

Rickard did some prospecting, but for most of the next seven years he ran gambling halls in the Yukon country, along the Klondike, and wherever else prospectors gathered, building a reputation for ability and honesty as a gambler. His interest in boxing came from the practice of using prize fights to attract patrons to saloons and gambling establishments.

Rickard was running a Nevada gambling house when he arranged his first big boxing match; it was a promotion for the town of Goldfield pitting lightweight champion Joe Gans against Battling Nelson on Labor Day, 1906. His success led Rickard to try for the Johnson-Jeffries bout, but he had to compete with several other promoters because of the overwhelming public interest in the defeat of Jack Johnson by a white fighter. The retired heavyweight champion, James J. Jeffries, was the logical challenger; he bragged that no one had ever knocked him down. Undefeated since winning the title from Bob Fitzsimmons in 1899, Joe Choynski had held him to a 20-round draw.

Rickard, the successful bidder, built a San Francisco arena before reformers forced a move to Nevada. Former champions "Gentleman Jim" Corbett and the "Boston Strong Boy," John L. Sullivan, were among Jeffries' supporters, and writers Jack London and Rex Beach were present at Reno to report the July 4, 1910 fight. Some 15,000—including eastern socialites who came on chartered trains and millionaire Ned Green of Terrell, who made the journey in his private railroad car—saw Johnson floor Jeffries three times in the fifteenth round before Referee "Tex" Rickard declared Johnson to be the winner and still champion. The reaction in several cities—mainly northern—was catastrophic; race riots between disappointed whites and exuberant blacks resulted in at least a dozen deaths and hundreds of injuries.

With $400,000 he had saved, Rickard tried to buy a Texas ranch, but finding prices too high he acquired five million acres in Paraguay on which he grazed 50,000 cattle. He prospered, made many Paraguayan friends, and met Theodore Roosevelt, who was exploring that country.

When "Tex" Rickard returned from South America in April, 1915, he learned that Jess Willard had taken Jack Johnson's heavyweight title and that some states had repealed their laws prohibiting prize fights. He leased Madison Square Garden for a match between Willard who stood 6-feet, 6-inches and weighed 252, and the 202-pound Frank Moran. Willard won easily and agreed—for a $100,000 fee—to meet any contender Rickard selected. Rickard signed the 180-pound Jack Dempsey to fight Willard on July 4 in Toledo. Surprised by the apparent interest, Rickard had an arena built to seat 80,000 people; however, an extended heat wave and other factors reduced

—Library of Congress

Billy Jordan introduces Jack Johnson at Reno, Nevada, on July 4, 1910. Promoter "Tex" Rickard, at right, was also the referee.

the number of spectators to fewer than 20,000. As was usually the case when the title changed hands, the champion did not train as hard as the challenger and came to the ring out of condition. In the first round Dempsey broke Willard's cheekbone and knocked him down several times. When Willard did not come out for the fourth round, the hardhitting Dempsey became the new heavyweight champion.

In 1920, Rickard took a ten year lease on Madison Square Garden, paying $350,000 a year. (This was the second Garden; the original had been razed in 1889.) Although designed by celebrated architect Stanford White, the much admired Garden, on the corner of Madison Square, was not profitable; however, Rickard believed boxing would change this—New York had recently legalized prize fights—and circus owner John Ringling concurred and backed Rickard.

In the seven years Jack Dempsey held the title Rickard promoted most of his bouts. Since Dempsey was not a popular champion Rickard realized that a match with Georges Carpentier would have great appeal; Americans were pro-French in 1921 and Carpentier had been a hero in the Army of France. He was not the best of the contenders, but he had style, in the ring and out. Promising Dempsey $300,000 and Carpentier $200,000, Rickard built a Jersey City arena to seat 91,000 people. It was the first fight ever broadcast, and the gate was a record $1.5 million as Dempsey whipped the Frenchman. In 1923 Dempsey met Argentina's Luis Angel Firpo in New York's Polo Grounds before 88,000 patrons. Firpo, the "Wild Bull of the Pampas," knocked the champion out of the ring in the first round, but Dempsey won in the second.

Rickard had done well in his ventures. Madison Square Garden was making money but was outdated, so he opened a new, $5.6-million Madison Square Garden—a mile away from Madison Square—in 1925. In the meantime, before 120,747 spectators at Philadelphia's Sesquicentennial Stadium, Gene Tunney won Jack Dempsey's title. Rickard scheduled a rematch, and in the fall of 1927, 104,903 fans—who had paid $2.6 million—saw Tunney again defeat Dempsey at Soldiers Field in Chicago.

"Tex" Rickard died in Miami, Florida, on January 6, 1929. His body was brought back to Madison Square Garden, where thousands of New Yorkers, in bitter cold, lined 8th Avenue and filed by his coffin. Streets were clogged, and 300 policemen maintained order while 9,000 attended the funeral and others stood on rooftops to view the procession.

—*Western History Department, Denver Public Library*

Billy Jordan introduces former champion James J. Jeffries, the "Great White Hope," at
Reno, Nevada, on July 4, 1910.

Jeffries had had to drop about 80 of his 300 pounds before the fight, and Johnson beat him badly.

—*Library of Congress*

At Havana, Cuba, on April 5, 1915, the huge Jess Willard knocked out Jack Johnson. The position of Johnson's arm—apparently shading his eyes—was taken by some as evidence that he was not really unconscious.

Moman Pruiett Successfully Defended 342 Capital Cases

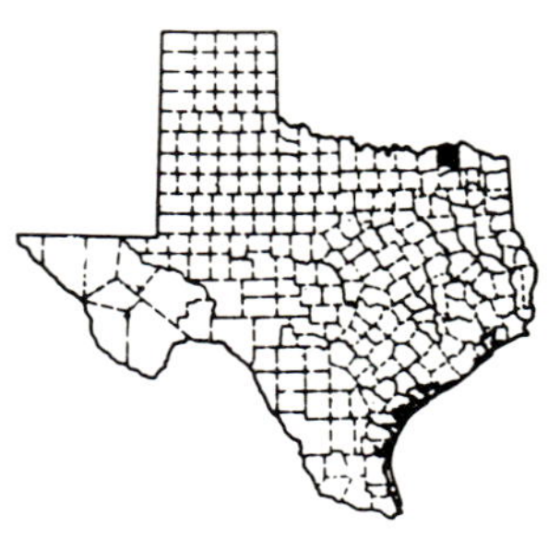

Moorman Pruiett was born July 12, 1872, aboard a boat on the Ohio River while his parents were moving westward in search of opportunity; finding very little, they barely scraped out a living in Missouri and Arkansas. Moorman shined shoes on the streets of Rogers and Hackett City, Arkansas, and because his mother wanted him to become a lawyer he cleaned the offices of Brewer and Hale for the privilege of reading law with them. At sixteen, Pruiett was given a two-year prison sentence for forgery; he had been unjustly convicted of raising figures on railroad freight bills he was hired to collect and keeping the difference. He served six months in the Little Rock penitentiary.

The Pruietts moved to Paris, Texas, and ran a boarding house; there Moorman was the janitor in Colonel Jake Hodges' law office in return for the use of his library. He had impressed Hodges and others with his brilliance when—largely because of the prior conviction—he was sent to prison for a robbery he did not commit. Regular visits by his mother to Governor Culberson resulted in his release in 1894 after serving two years. When a Moorman relative wrote Mrs. Pruiett that her son had disgraced the family, he changed his name to Moman. Moman Pruiett had been home a few months and was working in a warehouse—the only job he could get because of his record—when Judge David E. Bryant, of Sherman, stopped him on the street one evening, said he was aware of Pruiett's exceptional legal knowledge, and indicated that he believed Pruiett innocent of the crimes for which he had served time. He gave Pruiett $20, told him to buy a suit, and come to court. Pruiett obeyed, and Judge Bryant enrolled the 23-year-old Moman Pruiett as an attorney of the United States District Court; one interesting result was that the judge who had sentenced him to prison felt compelled to admit Pruiett to practice in the state courts. Thus began the career of one of the nation's most successful criminal lawyers. Pruiett represented 342 murder defendants, won acquittals for 304, and got sentences of from four years to life for 38; the sole death sentence assessed any of his clients was commuted by President McKinley. When Pruiett was admitted to practice before the United States Supreme Court, Senator Charles Culberson—who, as Texas governor, had commuted his sentence—was present to see him take the oath.

Pruiett married Lilly Belle Thrasher at Paris, and at the solicitation of Sam Garvin, he moved to Pauls Valley, Indian Territory. His reputation grew to the extent that when statehood came, a county was to be named for him, but Charles Haskell—who would become governor—objected, and Moman County became Creek County. When Edna Ferber wrote her novel, *Cimmaron*, she used as models for Yancey Cravat, her protagonist, Moman Pruiett and Temple Houston. Sam Houston's son, Temple, was born in the Texas governor's mansion shortly before General Houston was removed from office for refusal to swear allegiance to the Confederacy. Temple Houston was district attorney and state senator from the Texas Panhandle before moving to Woodward, Indian Territory. He was an able lawyer and was equally proficient with a six shooter.

In October, 1902, Pruiett was serving as a special prosecutor in an Enid case wherein

—Western History Collections, University of Oklahoma Library

Moman Pruiett, perhaps the nation's most effective criminal lawyer, was admitted to practice after twice having been unjustly convicted of crimes and having served time in Little Rock, Arkansas, and Huntsville, Texas, penitentiaries.

John Riggins was charged with murdering Harry F. Sears. Houston was Riggins' attorney, and the local newspaper reported that:

> Mr. Pruiett made the closing argument....His fiery zeal caused him to tread on the blunt toes of the figurative Houston boot. He told the jury that "the defendant's lawyer, who wore buckskins and twisted his hair up like a multitude of rats' tails, had but one virtue and claim to fame, and that was the undying reputation of an illustrious father." He shook his fist under Houston's nose and cried, "Spawn of the tee-pee!"

Pruiett, having gone too far, realized that Houston might very well kill him. That evening he took his pistol as he went down to the bar in the old Frantz Hotel. Houston came in and pretended not to see Pruiett. (According to Pruiett, Houston's buckskin coat collar was "foul from the grease of his long black hair, which he saturated and twisted into tight rolls, Indian fashion.") Houston said to a friend, "The young gentleman from the Chickasaw country is a pretty talker. He makes a pretty speech."

Meeting Houston's eyes, Pruiett said nothing. "I guess you have heard that Riggins is at liberty," Houston added.

Still staring at Pruiett, he asked, "Would the young gentleman from the Chickasaw country condescend to drink with the son of the immortal emancipator of Texas—the one who wears his hair on his coat collar like a multitude of rats' tails?"

Years later Pruiett wrote of what happened then:

> "The young gentleman from the Chickasaw country confines his professional feelings to the courtroom. He tries to give satisfaction to those who trust him enough to employ him. When he has done that he is able to look any man in the face, even his adversary, without an apology. He would be glad to drink with Temple Houston, an able lawyer."

> Houston weighed the remarks briefly and gave a quick nod of approval. "He is indeed a pretty speaker," he murmured. He raised his glass and the drinks were tossed off. Each nodding, they moved away from each other; neither changed the focus of the intense eye-to-eye gaze. Pruiett moved toward the exit....Pruiett left Enid on the midnight train. Houston dropped into a barber shop on the square next morning and he left his greasy curls. During the balance of his stormy career he wore his hair close-cropped, in cowboy fashion.

Sam Houston's youngest son, Temple, was the speaker at the dedication of the new capitol in Austin. Edna Ferber, in *Cimmaron*, modelled her protagonist after Temple Houston and Moman Pruiett.

Lillie Langtry Came to Her Town

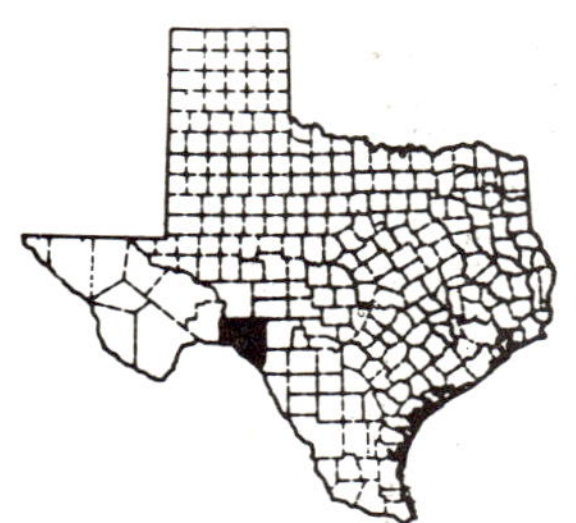

The town of Langtry was probably named for a railroad man—or Judge Roy Bean may, as he claimed, have given it the name of the English actress Lillie Langtry. At any rate the actress believed him when he told her it was her town; smitten after seeing her photograph, Bean called his saloon "The Jersey Lily" and invited her to come to Langtry. She did visit the town a few months after Bean's death in March, 1903—he had attended a San Antonio rooster fight and overimbibed—and she was given Roy Bean's six shooter as a souvenir.

Born on the Island of Jersey in 1852, Emilie Charlotte Le Breton said she was called "Lillie" because of her white skin. After she became a famous actress and married Langtry her friends included Oscar Wilde, who wrote poetry for her, James Whistler, who painted her, and Queen Victoria's sons, Prince Leopold and the future King Edward. Prime Minister Gladstone read Shakespeare to her. Earlier, when she toured the United States her leading man, Charles Coghlan, died and was buried at Galveston. Mrs. Langtry noted that the water covering Galveston in the 1900 storm "invaded the cemetery and swept many of the coffins (including that of Charles Coghlan) out to sea, which singular happening to his remains was predicted for him by a crystal-gazer while he was still a young man."

Of Roy Bean's invitation to visit Langry during that tour, she wrote:

> It was at the moment impossible, and on writing him my regrets, I offered to present an ornamental drinking fountain as a sop; but Roy Bean's quick reply was that it would be quite useless, as the only thing the citizens of Langtry did not drink was water.

This was Mrs. Langtry's account of her 1903 visit to Langtry:

> The afternoon sun was blazing down on the parched sandy plain, with its monotonous clotting of sage-brush and low growing cactus, when the Sunset Express came to a sudden stop. A casual glance from the window...revealed no reason why we should pause there...we were actually at Langtry, but on account of my car being, as usual, placed at the tail end of the long train, we could see no sign of habitation. I hurriedly alighted, just as a cloud of sand heralded the approach of a numerous throng of citizens ploughing their way along the entire length of the train to give me the "glad hand."
>
> Justice of the Peace Dodd, a quiet interesting man, introduced himself, and then presented Postmaster Fielding, Stationmaster Smith, and other persons of consequence. Next in order came a number of cowboys...garbed in their finest leathers and most flamboyant shirts, as became the occasion, making a picturesque group, one loosing off his gun as he passed me, in tangible proof of his appreciation of my visit.
>
> Thirty or forty girls, all about fifteen or sixteen, followed, and were announced en bloc as "the young ladies of Langtry," and, finally, "our wives" brought up the rear.
>
> The special concession allowed by the railway authorities being limited to half an hour, I was regretfully unable to see the town proper, which lay across the line and some distance from the tiny wooden shed with "LANGTRY" writ large upon it, and which did duty for the station, but happily the Jersey Lilly Saloon was near at hand, and we trudged to it

Famed English actress Lillie Langtry made a couple of triumphant tours to the United States where Judge Roy Bean claimed to have named Langtry, Texas for her.

through sage-brush and prickly cactus.

I found it a roughly built wooden two storey house, its entire front being shaded by a piazza, on which a chained monkey gambolled....The interior of the "Ritz" of Langtry consisted of a long, narrow room, which comprised the entire ground floor, whence a ladder staircase led to a sleeping-loft. One side of the room was given up to a bar....The tables showed plainly that they had been severely used, for they were slashed as if with bowie-knives, and on each was a well-thumbed deck of playing cards. It was here that Roy Bean... used to hold his court....

We still had a few minutes to see the schoolhouse, which was adjacent to the saloon, but the schoolmistress had sensibly locked the door on this great holiday, so after pledging to send a supply of suitable books from San Francisco I returned to the train. The cemetery was pointed out to me in the distance and the significant fact deduced that only fifteen of the citizens buried there had died natural deaths.

One of the officials, a large, red-bearded, exuberant person, confided to a lady of my company that he deplored not having brought me a keg of freshmade butter, also that he had a great mind to kiss me, only he didn't know how I would take it, and I thankfully add that Miss Leila Repton had the presence of mind to put a damper on his bold design.

On nearing the train, which was becoming rather impatient, I saw the strange sight of a huge cinnamon bear careening across the line, dragging a cowboy at the end of a long chain....I had acquired a jumping frog at Charleston, an alligator in Florida, a number of horned toads, and a delightfully tame prairie dog called Bob. Hence, I suppose, the correct inference was drawn that I was fond of animals, and the boys resolved to add the late Roy Bean's pet to my collection. They hoisted the unwilling animal onto the platform, and tethered him to the rail, but happily, before I had time to rid myself of this unwelcome addition without seeming discourteous, he broke away, scattering the crowd and causing some of the vaqueros to start shooting wildly at all angles.

Mrs. Langtry took some resurrection plants with her. "The dried up, withered little plants preserve the germ of life even if baked in the oven, and after any lapse of time will recover their verdure...." In England, she gave one to the American painter, John Singer Sargent, who responded, "That resurrection-plant is amazing. It is a green tree today."

Lillie Langtry was unable to visit Langtry during Judge Bean's lifetime, but did so after his death.

Alfalfa Bill Murray Designed the Oklahoma Constitution

Bill Murray was born at Toadsuck community, near Collinsville, Grayson County, Texas, on November 21, 1869. After receiving very little formal education, he passed an examination for a first-grade teacher's certificate. While teaching in Parker County, he became interested in politics and met Jim Hogg, who would be his hero. Moving to Navarro County, he acquired a reputation as a speaker in debates with members of the upstart People's Party. In 1892 he ran for the State Senate against O. B. Colquitt, who would later become governor, and George Jester, who would be lieutenant governor. Jester won, and two years later Colquitt defeated Murray for the same office.

Murray was admitted to the bar in 1897, started to practice in Fort Worth, and then moved to Tishomingo, the Chickasaw capital, where he assisted Indians in getting on the tribal rolls and was the Chickasaw Nation's legal advisor. He married the governor's niece, Mary Alice Hearrell, and their first son was born on the first day of the twentieth century. The second, Johnston, was named for Chickasaw governor Douglas Johnston and would later become governor of Oklahoma.

Murray lived in a log house on a Twelve Mile Prairie farm, where he carried out agricultural experiments. His enthusiasm for alfalfa resulted in his nickname. Murray spent much of his time studying law and government in preparation for the time when statehood would come. He was active in a number of organizations, including the Democratic party.

At that time the eastern part of present Oklahoma was the Indian Territory and the western portion was Oklahoma Territory. The people of the Indian Territory did not want to join the Oklahoma Territory as a single state. In 1905 Murray attended the Muskogee convention to transform the Indian Territory into the state of Sequoyah. Murray, who knew more about constitutions than anyone else, brought with him copies of the basic documents of Australia, Switzerland, and New Zealand. He played a major role in the convention, and the proposed constitution reflected his belief in government controlled by small farmers. Although citizens voted overwhelmingly for the Sequoyah constitution, Congress and President Theodore Roosevelt insisted that the two territories form one state.

The Oklahoma statehood enabling act having become law, a constitutional convention met at Guthrie in November, 1906; the resulting document was quite similar to the Sequoyah constitution. Bill Murray, the presiding officer, was an ex officio member of each of the convention's 45 committees, all of which were appointed by him. One of the new state's 75 counties was named for Murray, and Roger Q. Mills County honored the presiding officer's old Corsicana friend. Among the famous men invited to speak to the convention were Quanah Parker, Theodore Roosevelt, and Robert La Follette. Will Rogers attended some of the sessions with his father, Clem, after whom Rogers County was named.

The Republicans imported William Howard Taft to argue against the constitution, which Democrat William Jennings Bryan called the best in the Union. It was adopted by a vote of 180,333 to 73,059, and on November 16, 1907, Oklahoma became the 46th state. It was a rural state of 1.5 million people and 200,000 farmers; only five towns had 10,000 or more citizens.

"Alfalfa Bill" Murray, on the right, dictates to his secretary in his front porch office at Tishomingo.

Bill Murray Became Governor of Oklahoma

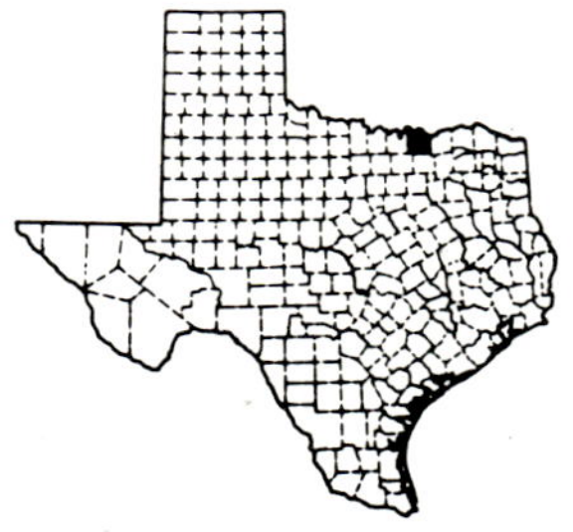

When Oklahoma's first legislature met, in late 1907, Democrat Bill Murray was the first speaker. He lost his bid to become governor in 1910, but was elected to Congress in the next election. As chairman of the Oklahoma delegation, Murray was instrumental in obtaining the Democratic nomination for Woodrow Wilson. Some of the representatives who entered Congress with Murray were Kentucky's Alben Barkley, who would be Harry Truman's vice president; Sam Rayburn, of Texas, later Speaker of the House; Cordell Hull, of Tennessee, and James Byrnes, of South Carolina, each of whom became Secretary of State; and Virginia's influential Carter Glass.

After Murray again failed to become governor, in 1918, he established a colony in Bolivia, which failed. Penniless, he borrowed $40 and announced his gubernatorial candidacy soon after the October, 1929, stock market crash. He stated that "the poor and weak shall have my especial care, for the rich and strong can usually protect themselves." His was a "cheese and crackers campaign." Without a car, he hitched rides over the state. The slight support he received came from the farmers and the poor. He did not seem to be a significant factor until he bested some strong opposition in the first Democratic primary. In the run-off his millionaire opponent, Frank Buttram, stated that "the man has been a failure all his life." But Murray won easily. To assist him in the general election, Murray got Thomas P. Gore, an old friend from Corsicana, to run for the Senate again. As candidates of the poor, he and the blind senator were unbeatable. Murray said:

> I made but one political promise during that campaign. A friend of mine from the northern part of the State took a lot of time and spent considerable money on gas and oil that he might help me to make my speaking engagements....I felt that he deserved a promise of some kind of reward; so I told him if he ever got into trouble and got into the penitentiary while I was Governor that I'd pardon him.

Murray's inauguration on January 12, 1931, was in character; the oath of office was administerd by his 91-year-old father, Uriah Dow Murray, a notary public and sometime Holiness preacher, who said, "Many's the time I've preached to more folks than this." Murray told the crowd, "You know the old boy don't see so well as he used to," and began his inaugural address. It was a cold, raw day but 12,000 enthusiastic spectators attended the outdoors ceremonies.

To deal with the problem of oil overproduction—which caused the price to fall to 22¢ a barrel and resulted in the inability to recover thousands of barrels by wasting gas needed to raise petroleum to the surface—Murray called out the national guard. Designating a fifty-foot martial law area around each of the state's 3,106 oil wells he closed down all of them. Production would not be permitted until corrective steps, such as the passage of a petroleum conservation act, were taken.

Murray also used the national guard in a controversy with Texas over the Red River free bridges. For many years the privately-owned toll bridges had had a monopoly.

"Alfalfa Bill" Murray, as governor of Oklahoma, signs into law the Firemen's Pension Bill in the presence of sponsors and firemen.

Then when Texas and Oklahoma built three bridges across Red River—at Ryan, Oklahoma, Gainesville, Texas, and Denison, Texas—the toll bridge owners got injunctions against Texas to keep the free bridges closed; the court was enforcing a contract by which Texas had granted an exclusive right to operate bridges across Red River. Alfalfa Bill Murray's position was that since Oklahoma had not made such a contract, it was free to operate the public bridges. Although enjoined by a federal court, Murray ordered the Oklahoma Highway Patrol to open the free bridges. Texas governor Ross Sterling had Rangers at the south ends of the bridges, keeping them closed in obedience to the court order. Murray had the Oklahoma Highway Department plow up the roads leading from the toll bridges, so they could not be used; he declared martial law around the free bridges, and the Oklahoma National Guard opened them to traffic. As more injunctions were issued, Murray said, "I have instructed my military officers to arrest any federal judge, United States marshal or any other official who attempts to take charge of the situation." Because of his long study of constitutional law, Murray knew that he could act boldly in this situation without fear of embarrassment. As to Texas and the Rangers he told his militia, "You fellows be easy on Mr. Sterling's Rangers; don't be too rough. Just take their guns and tobacco and give them a light kick in the pants if you have to." On the equities of the case he stated:

> In the first place there is nothing in our contract with Texas that divided our ownership of the bridges at the middle of the river. I think we are entitled to claim that we own a half that might be divided squarely in the middle of the passage and running clear across....In the second place, the Texas officials may have never seen the old Spanish Grant that originally defined the border of Texas. It is on the South—or "right" bank of the Red River, and that would place all of the bridges in Oklahoma.

There was never any doubt as to who was governor during Murray's years. Promising to veto certain bills after their sponsors had threatened him, he said, "...if you've got any impeachment ideas in your heads, hop to it. It'll be like a bunch of rabbits tryin' to get a wildcat out of a hole." He pressed for free textbooks for the public schools but begrudged the money spent on higher education; he charged that the colleges turned out "high-toned bums."

Bill Murray made a respectable effort to get the Democratic presidential nomination in 1932, but Franklin Roosevelt was too strong. Leaving office in 1933, Bill Murray retired to a small farm near Idabel where he and Mrs. Murray lived in a four-room, unpainted shack and, owning no car, he hitchhiked whenever he needed to go anywhere.

—*Western History Collections, University of Oklahoma Library*

"Alfalfa Bill" Murray ordered the Oklahoma National Guard to keep the three Texas-Oklahoma free bridges open to traffic despite federal marshals and Texas Rangers.

John Pliska Built Texas' First Airplane

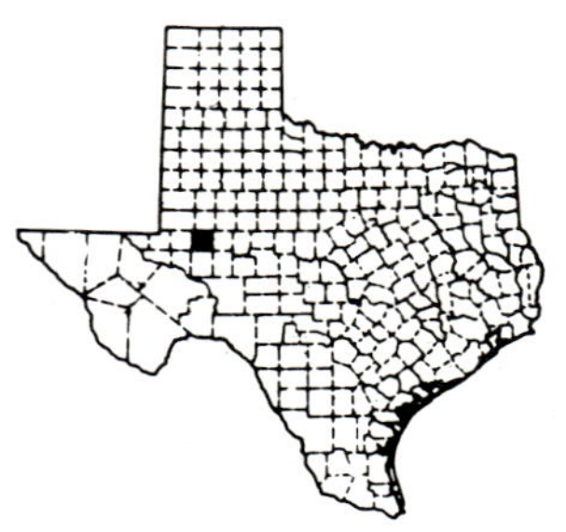

In 1903 the Ford Motor Company was organized, the first trans-continental automobile trip was made—it required almost two and a half months—and on December 17, Wilbur and Orville Wright made their first flight at Kitty Hawk, North Carolina. John Pliska, a Midland blacksmith, was terribly excited by the news; as a soldier in Europe he had taken training in handling observation balloons and was fascinated by the idea of flight. He began drawing plans and accumulating materials as early as 1909, but his efforts to build a flying machine proceeded no further until he saw his first airplane.

In 1910, newspaper millionaire William Randolph Hearst offered $50,000 to the first man to fly across the United States. Of eight entrants only two finished: Robert G. Fowler and C.P. Rodgers. Rodgers left New York on September 17, 1911, and followed the railroad to Pasadena, California, arriving on November 5, after crashing at least 12 times; he was the first to fly the country from east to west. Fowler made the first flight from west to east, and when he landed his plane at Midland on November 19, 1911, John Pliska was among the spectators.

Pliska and his good friend, Gray Coggin, were thrilled; they had to own such a machine. Rationalizing their desires, they decided that an airplane in West Texas, where few people had seen one, would earn substantial sums at public events, so they set out to build one. John Pliska had come from Czechoslovakia in 1897, and he and John Hundle, his brother-in-law, had opened a blacksmith shop in 1908. Coggin had been the Midland-to-Carlsbad, New Mexico, mail driver; this was a difficult assignment because of lack of roads, poor automobiles, and a dearth of garages and service stations. By 1911 Coggin was rancher Henry Halff's chauffeur and mechanic.

They devoted their evening hours to the airplane, using part of the blacksmith shop, exhausting their savings, and borrowing from friends and families. Mrs. Pliska worried about the expenditure of time and money and feared that her husband might be killed in the vehicle. As her daughter, Mary Beth, so beautifully put it:

> She told Uncle John that she could look out of the window of their home, which was located on South Loraine Street, and see my father and Mr. Coggin across the railroad track working on and testing the aeroplane after it had been built. When my uncle received these letters from my mother he told his father about them and my grandfather told Uncle John to write my mother and tell her that he felt my father should stay on the ground and make a living for his family, because he could not make a living in the air.

Pliska and Coggin had a difficult task; men were still learning how to make airplanes, and much trial and error was being practiced. They modeled their craft on the pusher-type biplane designed by Glenn Curtiss. When they were ready for an engine, Pliska and Coggin hired out on a cattle train and worked their way northward to Sandusky, Ohio, where the Roberts Motor Company manufactured power plants for airplanes. They bought a four-cylinder engine and spent several weeks learning about it and buying other materials. The motor developed about 40 horsepower, weighed 165 pounds,

Blacksmith John Pliska stands beside the airplane he and Grey Coggin—at the controls—constructed in Midland in 1911.

and cost $1,500, payable in installments. It ran on a special fuel, which was quite expensive because it had to be shipped from New York.

In the spring of 1912, the plane, ready to be flown, was hauled by wagon to a field which had very little mesquite. They could get the plane off the ground, but it would not remain airborne; Pliska and Coggin decided the fabric covering offered too much air resistance, for instead of balloon silk they had used canvass—which was less expensive, but heavier—for the wings. Although shellacking the surfaces added weight—with pilot and full radiator and fuel tank, the plane weighed 750 pounds—it reduced the drag sufficiently to solve the problem.

As they learned more about flight they made changes which improved the airplane's performance, but still they were not satisfied; the motor would not deliver 1,400 revolutions per minute, as guaranteed. The company claimed Midland's 2,800-foot elevation caused the difficulty and contended that the engine would perform properly at sea level.

Mrs. Pliska's reservations about the airplane increased as her husband and Coggin suffered a series of minor accidents in perfecting the craft and improving their flying techniques. The flights were made from Henry Halff's polo field. (General John J. Pershing was one of those who played polo there.) At a July 4, 1912, celebration at Odessa Pliska could not get off the ground for more than a short distance, and some spectators demanded refunds. Obviously they could not make the monthly payments with unhappy audiences. They returned the engine to the manufacturer and hoisted the rest of the plane to the ceiling of the blacksmith shop; there it remained, undisturbed for half a century, until the building was torn down. The children of John Pliska—who had died in 1956—gave the airplane to the City of Midland, and the Abell-Hanger Foundation obtained a Roberts engine and built a museum for the restored plane at the Midland Air Terminal.

Pliska and Coggin believed their inability to remain airborne was because of the engine's inadequate power and returned it to the manufacturer. They stored the rest of the airplane in Pliska's blacksmith shop temporarily; when the shop was torn down fifty years later, John Pliska's children gave the plane to the City of Midland. The Abell-Hanger Foundation obtained a motor and constructed a display case for the airplane at the Midland airport.

Black Jack Pershing Led a Punitive Expedition into Mexico

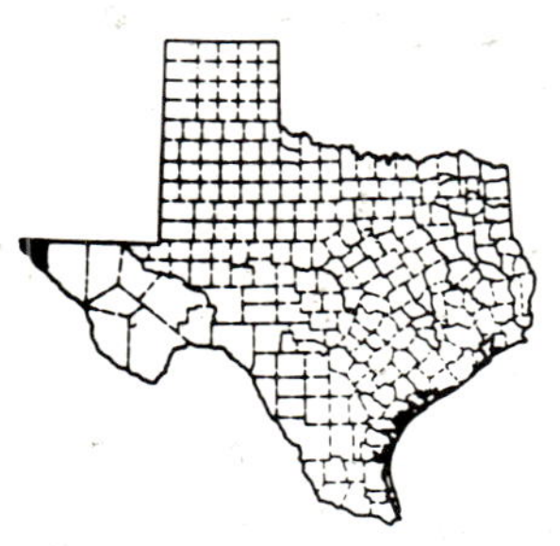

John J. Pershing, of Laclede, Missouri, who wanted to be a lawyer, attended West Point because he could not afford college; the military academy offered a good, free education. He was almost 22 when he entered; some of his classmates were only sixteen. Pershing graduated 30th in a class of 77—General William Tecumseh Sherman conferred his degree—and was commissioned a lieutenant of cavalry in 1886. Twice he served with the 10th Cavalry, a Negro regiment he considered his "home outfit" and the source of his nickname, "Black Jack." While he was the instructor of military science and tactics at the University of Nebraska he taught mathematics—Willa Cather and Dorothy Canfield Fisher were among his students—graduated from the law school, and was licensed as a Nebraska attorney. As a 38-year-old lieutenant, he was teaching at West Point when he met Theodore Roosevelt, and later Roosevelt used the very able Pershing as an example of why Army promotions should not be strictly controlled by seniority.

Pershing distinguished himself in the Spanish-American War and in the Philippines' Moro troubles. Since Congress still had not given Roosevelt power to reward by promotion company-grade and field-grade Army officers—he could only raise officers to general rank—the president made the 46-year-old Captain Pershing a brigadier general. In one mighty leap Pershing had passed 862 officers who were senior to him on the promotion list. Because he had married the daughter of Senator Francis Warren, of Wyoming, the chairman of the Armed Forces Committee, critics suggested favoritism, but Roosevelt pointed out that he had made speeches citing Pershing's plight well before the soldier met Miss Warren.

Pershing was commanding the 8th Infantry Brigade at the Presidio in San Francisco when he was ordered to Fort Bliss in April, 1914. Mexico had been in chaos since Porfirio Diaz's long dictatorial tenure was ended by revolution in 1911. His successor, Francisco Madero, had been killed by General Victoriano Huerta, who then became president. Ten days later Woodrow Wilson was inaugurated for his first term; Wilson said, "I will not recognize a government of butchers." An incident resulted in Wilson's sending an occupation force to Vera Cruz and moving Pershing's 6th and 16th Infantry regiments from the Presidio to the Mexican border at El Paso in preparation for an invasion. When Huerta fled and was succeeded by Carranza there was no need for American intervention. Pershing would simply patrol the border to discourage the bandits who raided into Texas and to keep the armies of Villa and Obregon south of the Río Grande. In an effort to avoid hostilities, Pershing cultivated the Mexican generals. Villa liked the attention he got from the American newspapers; in 1911, he delayed his capture of Juárez after realizing that the opening of the World Series would have the attention of the American public for the next few days. Pershing was suspicious of Villa, although he believed Obregon was sincere.

In August, 1915, a week before Pershing's wife and four children were to join him in El Paso, a fire at their Presidio quarters took the lives of all but six-year-old Warren Pershing. Returning to El Paso after the funerals, Pershing was informed that Villa was

General John J. Pershing tried to avoid border problems by cultivating General Obregon, left, and Pancho Villa. This meeting occurred prior to Villa's Columbus raid.

causing trouble. Rumor had it that Germany was financing Villa; if the Americans had enough other troubles they could not help England and France. Villa and Carranza had become enemies and were trying to destroy each other; Wilson recognized the government of President Venustiano Carranza and, while keeping supplies from Villa, allowed arms and ammunition to reach Carranza's forces. In addition, Mexican troops were permitted to come into the United States, go by train to Douglas, Arizona, and reinforce Agua Prieta in anticipation of Villa's attack; whether or not Villa knew about this, in general he felt he deserved better than the United States was giving him.

On March 7, 1916, came word that 1,000 of Villa's bandits were camped across the border from Columbus, New Mexico, a railroad town about 75 miles from El Paso where 21 officers and 532 men of the 13th Cavalry had been stationed for five years, guarding the international boundary. It appeared that the Mexicans were moving eastward, so the Americans were surprised when the Villistas attacked early in the morning of March 9; they retired about dawn leaving seven American soldiers and eight civilians dead and thirteen soldiers and civilians wounded. The raiders had attacked any building showing a light and invaded any place promising loot; they took all the valuables they could find, including wedding rings. Sixty-seven of the Villistas were killed on the American side of the border, and some cavalry pursued the raiders 15 miles into Mexico and killed 75 to 100 more.

American complaints to Mexico City made it clear that Carranza's government did not have the power to prevent another such attack. The Mexican president declared that he wanted Villa's band destroyed and asked that:

> Mexican forces be permitted to cross into American territory in pursuit of the aforementioned bandits led by Villa, upon the understanding that, reciprocally, the forces of the United States may cross into Mexican Territory if the raid effected at Columbus should unfortunately be repeated at any other point on the border.

As Pershing stated later, Carranza had as much control over the border as if he "lived in London." Secretary of War Newton Baker ordered an expedition into Mexico to capture Villa and halt further aggressions by him.

Pershing was given the difficult task of operating in foreign territory in such fashion as to not provoke a war. The Army was in a pitiful condition; the quartermaster was only beginning to utilize truck transport, and while aircraft was being used extensively in the European war, the United States had a handful of primitive planes which promptly fell apart in Mexico. Pershing's worst problem was what disposition to make of Villa if he should be caught; there would be trouble, perhaps war, if Villa were punished, and should he be captured and not made to answer for the murders at Columbus, Americans would be outraged.

A week after the Columbus attack Pershing took two fast-moving cavalry columns into Mexico. Accompanying him was his old outfit, the 10th Cavalry, his aide, First Lieutenant George S. Patton, Jr., and a contingent of Apache scouts, some of whom had served in the Geronimo campaigns years before. Villa's forces were scattered; Villa himself was hiding while he recovered from a painful leg wound inflicted by one of his unwilling "volunteers." In early May, bandits from across the Río Grande raided two towns in the Big Bend country, and about 5,000 National Guardsmen were activated and sent to the border. The 8th Cavalry, at Fort Bliss, entered Mexico below Boquillas and followed the bandits 200 miles into the interior, killing several and capturing some. The rest of the Regular Army was on the border within a few weeks, and as

After Pancho Villa invaded Columbus, New Mexico, Pershing was orderd to pursue him into Mexico. This river crossing was staged for press purposes, Pershing earlier having entered Mexico by staff car.

more incidents occurred almost the entire National Guard was ordered to the Río Grande.

The last element of Pershing's expedition left Mexico in February, 1917, two months before our entry into World War I. El Paso honored Pershing with a parade and banquet. In the meantime Villa had recovered and was sacking Mexican towns. Richard O'Connor wrote:

> The expedition into Chihuahua was a rigorous field test for almost the entire Regular Army, as well as 150,000 National Guardsmen. Without that experience the first divisions sent to France could hardly have performed as well as they did.

Of some 10,000 who took part in Pershing's punitive expedition were future generals Courtney Hodges, William Simpson, Lesley McNair, U.S. Grant, III, Brehon B. Somervell, Carl Spaatz, Millard Harmon and Ralph Royce.

Two weeks after his return Pershing succeeded Major General Frederick Funston, who died of a heart attack, as commander of the southern department of the Army. Pershing was at San Antonio when he was given command of the American Expeditionary Force, which was to be sent to France. After discovery of the Zimmerman telegram proposing that Mexico, as Germany's ally, attack the United States, for which Mexico would receive Texas, California and other territory, Americans resigned themselves to fighting a war.

The expedition into Mexico provided valuable experience for Pershing, who was still
in Texas when he was chosen to command the American Expeditionary Force in France.

Pershing Brought Chinese Refugees out of Mexico

The lot of the Chinese in Mexico had always been unfortunate; while they were free to become citizens, Chinese immigrants stirred antagonisms because of their energy and their failure to take sides in the revolutions. By trading with both—or all—of the parties striving for power, they offended everyone. Partisans viewed their neutrality as lack of patriotism. Edward Eugene Briscoe, in his superb thesis done at Saint Mary's University, noted that: "The Chinese reaped where they did not sow." Typical of harrassment visited upon them was that of the Sonoran revolutionary general who forbade more than four Chinese from residing in a house. They were not to visit each other for more than two days at a time, and they could not work as domestics, because those jobs were needed for widows created by the revolutions.

When Pershing led his punitive expedition into Mexico one week after the March 9, 1916, raid on Columbus, he found that many of Mexico's Chinese lived in towns along the northern border; although the Chinese exclusion acts kept them from entering the United States, they could live nearby. As they moved into the Mexican interior, American soldiers were amazed to meet Chinese peddlers, who sold them tobacco, matches, candy, fruit, and soap. The availability of these items was appreciated, for resentful Mexican merchants wanted nothing to do with the soldiers from the north.

After the first deep thrust, Pershing pulled back and made the Mormon settlement of Colonia Dublan—which lay 110 miles south of Columbus—his headquarters. Many Chinese, whose ill-treatment had been aggravated because of their commerce with the Americans, clustered about the Army posts for trade and protection. Briscoe explained that Chinese peddlers were the only source of many items. "Business was brisk; the buyer was appreciative; the seller profited; an enviable economic condition."

But Pancho Villa's threats constituted a license for anyone who chose to kill a Chinese. After the Chihuahua City garrison commander raised a Chinese militia company which routed his troops, Villa swore to hang every "Chino in northern Mexico." Many were killed and injured in Chihuahua and Durango riots; as atrocities continued the number of refugees increased.

As the United States was drawn more surely into the European War it was obvious that the 8,000 to 10,000 men in Mexico—the nation's only significant army—should be brought home. It was also obvious that the refugees would have to leave Mexico. Pershing and the last of his troops crossed the border on February 5, 1917, two days after President Woodrow Wilson severed diplomatic relations with Germany. The 3,800 refugees accompanying the Army included 527 Chinese men—no women. The exclusion laws—which originated in China's desire to keep her people at home and were retained to protect American laborers from competition—permitted only students, merchants, travelers, and government officials to enter; after some qualified under the exemptions and others went back to China, 427 remained in the Columbus refugee camp, where their subsistence was paid by American Chinese. They moved to San Antonio and worked for the Army during World War I. With General Pershing's support, in late 1921 the Congress provided for registration of the remaining 379 so they might become citizens; a few months later they were permitted to move out of the San Antonio refugee camp.

—Institute of Texan Cultures, San Antonio

After the Chinese refugees from Mexico spent several months in a New Mexico camp, they moved to San Antonio's Fort Sam Houston where they worked for the Army and lived in this camp until legislation permitted them to become citizens.

Masonic Home Was Located in Fort Worth

Texas Masons had always taken responsibility for orphans and widows of members; in earlier times they were placed in the homes of other Masons, but by the close of Reconstruction it was obvious that institutions were needed to serve those dependents. Among the many advantages of institutional care were: (1) more individuals could be served at a smaller per capita cost, (2) greater security could be afforded the orphan or widow by the thousands of Masons who would support an institution, (3) orphaned brothers and sisters would remain together, (4) health services would be far superior, and (5) children probably would be more independent people than if they were placed with foster families. The Grand Lodge of Texas, in 1848, began setting aside funds for educational purposes; over the years the objective was broadened to include the care and education of orphans and support of widows. As funds on hand approached the $100,000 goal they had established, the Masons began searching for a location. Eleven sites, including 300 acres near Texas A & M and 200 acres at Houston, were proposed in 1896. In the next year, the Grand Lodge chose Fort Worth in preference to a Temple site; Fort Worth had offered to donate 200 acres and $5,000 in cash and building materials.

The Widows and Orphans Fund having reached $124,000, in late 1898 a contract was let for the first building, which would cost $17,500—$100,000 was set aside as a permanent endowment. The building had a schoolroom, dormitory space for 50 children, quarters for the superintendent, a kitchen, and a dining hall. The home for widows and orphans was opened in October, 1899. It would provide the children with a common education as well as training in agriculture and mechanics.

The first superintendent was Dr. Frank Rainey, a Confederate surgeon and Texas legislator who had headed the School for the Blind for 21 years. About forty children were accepted; their support and education cost $188.13 apiece that first year. Funds came from endowment interest and whatever was left over from the operating income of the Grand Lodge. Enrollment was frozen after the Galveston storm because much money was needed for the relief of destitute survivors and for repairing the damaged temple of the Grand Lodge. That emergency demonstrated the lack of wisdom of depending upon the remnant of operating accounts for support of the home, so in 1901 the Masons committed 50¢ of each member's dues to the support of the institution. In 1917 this assessment was raised to $1.00 and later it became $1.75 per annum. Masonic Home's endowment fund of $7,746,415.50 was yielding nearly half a million dollars in 1972, and the cost of maintaining each student was about $3,000 a year.

The original building had no quarters for the 22 widows who applied. Although another dormitory, to accomodate 80 children and wives of deceased Masons, was completed in 1900, only one widow had been admitted. In 1911, when the Royal Arch Chapter opened its Home for Aged Masons, at Arlington, the 20 widows at the Fort Worth institution were moved there; their maintenance was paid by Masonic Widows and Orphans Home, which then became Masonic Orphans Home. R.L. Dillard, Jr.

The administration building occupies the site of the first building on the campus of Masonic Home and School.

noted that the orphans home paid $215,500 in behalf of the 71 widows at Arlington in 1971.

The Masonic Home Independent School District, created in 1913, operates a twelve-grade school and participates in the per capita allotment program of the state. Most instruction was vocational at first, but as time passed more academic work was offered.

The peak enrollment of 456 was reached in the depression year of 1930. While only orphans of Master Masons were eligible in the beginning, it was soon apparent that this policy was too restrictive. Now "needy children and grandchildren of Master Masons in Texas"—including adoptive children—are eligible. In the first half century some 2,000 children lived at Masonic Home and 720 graduated from the school. More than 300 served in the armed forces. In the decade following World War II, 67% of the graduates of Masonic Home High School went on to college, whereas the national average was 40%. Among the distinguished alumni of the school were: Dr. Blake Van Leer, who entered from Bonham, graduated in 1909, was an Army colonel, won the French Croix de Guerre in World War I, and became the president of Georgia Tech; Major General Charles Christenberry, a 1913 graduate who studied at T.C.U., Columbia, and Oxford, and was the Army Adjutant General of the Mediterranean Theater of Operations in World War II; and Dr. Abner McCall, who entered with his brother and sister in 1922 and remained at Masonic Home eleven years. Dr. McCall holds degrees from Baylor and the University of Michigan and was dean of the Baylor Law School and Associate Justice of the Texas Supreme Court prior to becoming president of Baylor University.

This handsome chapel dominates the quiet campus of Masonic Home.

Rusty Russell's Mighty Mites Were Giant-Killers

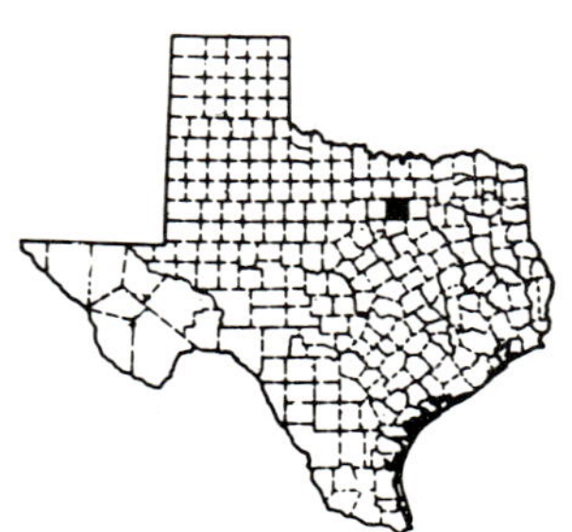

By 1932 the Great Depression had brought the nation to its knees; some 2,200 banks had failed the year before and twelve million men were without work. In Washington, bonus marchers—unemployed World War I veterans—gathered in such numbers that President Hoover ordered General Douglas MacArthur to disperse them. At Hopewell, New Jersey, Charles A. Lindbergh, Jr., was kidnapped and murdered; the case would remain unsolved until the 1934 arrest of Bruno Richard Hauptmann.

Most of the good news was in the sports pages. Babe Ruth and Lou Gehrig were leading the New York Yankees to a world's championship, and Beaumont's Mildred Didrikson was becoming history's greatest woman athlete. But Texas' big success story was Masonic Home's football team. With only eleven orphan boys—plus "the back substitute" and, sometimes, "the line substitute"—the Mighty Mites were beating the best teams in the state. Friday after Friday David abused Goliath, as Fort Worth's North Side Steers, Dallas' Woodrow Wilson Wildcats, and Amarillo's Golden Sandstorm fell before the Masons.

For those who wondered about such things the answer was simple: a football genius—a master handler of boys, H.N. (Rusty) Russell—was in residence at Masonic Home; he had come there almost by accident. Russell was coaching at Temple High School in 1927 when a friend, who had accepted the Masonic Home job, changed his mind and persuaded Russell to take the position so he could be released. There was no future for a Masonic Home coach; with never more than 85 boys in its four grades, the high school was a weak Class B. The real football was played in Class A.

From a standing start—Sherman beat the Masons 97-19 in 1927—Russell started to build. He could not recruit; students came to the home only by being orphaned. With so few boys Russell's teams would always be out-numbered and usually out-weighed, so his strategy was to out-plan, out-maneuver, and out-fight the opposition.

Russell began scheduling Class A teams, and before long his larger opponents—who thought they were arranging breathers—were rationalizing their losses as the results of a mythical 300 Mighty Mite plays. The Masons defeated so many big schools their fans believed they deserved to be in Class A, and when the undefeated 1931 team won its Class B region by beating Clarendon 55-0, Masons urged that the Mighty Mites be moved to the higher category in spite of the tiny high school enrollment. The Interscholastic League had no power to re-classify them, but the big Fort Worth district could invite them in, so in 1932 the Masons were voted into District 7A. That year they defeated all the Fort Worth schools—North Side 40-14, Polytechnic 18-0, Stripling 27-6, Central (which later became Paschal) 6-0—and beat Bridgeport 53-6, Weatherford 62-6, and Mineral Wells 19-6. They scored 224 points to their opponents' 32.

As winner of District 7A the Mighty Mites would play the Dallas champion, the Woodrow Wilson Wildcats. After observing that the starting elevens were evenly matched, the *Star-Telegram's* Amos Melton wrote of Masonic Home, "If one or two of

—Masonic Home and School

"Rusty" Russell used fewer than half of these boys during the undefeated 1932 season in which he lost the state championship to Corsicana, (0-0), on penetrations. His custom was to take as many boys as possible on game trips because, "They never got to go anywhere." Fourth from left on the back row is Baylor University president Abner McCall. Fourth from left, middle row, is District Judge Perry Pickett. Second from right, front row, is Allie White, three times All-State tackle and for many years a T.C.U. assistant coach.

their regulars are injured...they will be at a great disadvantage. Against Central, Russell used only twelve men.''

David O'Brien was Woodrow Wilson's quarterback, and I.B. Hale was a tackle; both would make All-American while leading Texas Christian University to a national championship. The Wildcats' major problem was Athletic Director P.C. Cobb's overwhelming desire to beat the Masons. Cobb—for whom the old Dal-Hi Stadium is named—sent coaches from the other Dallas high schools to scout Masonic Home and help Woodrow Wilson's great coach, Herschel Forrester, prepare for the game. Their huge mass of observations and instructions confused the players; there was simply too much to learn, so while the Wildcats were trying to remember what they were to do in a given situation the Mighty Mites were scoring touchdowns. Before 10,000 fans in T.C.U. Stadium, Masonic Home beat a fine—but over-coached—Woodrow Wilson, 40-7.

In the quarter-finals the Masons defeated Sherman's Bearcats, 20-0, on an icy field. Never in Texas Interscholastic League history had a Fort Worth team gone so far in the play-offs; their next opponent was Amarillo. In twelve games only two touchdowns had been scored against Blair Cherry's Golden Sandstorm.

The weather prior to the Amarillo game was bad. T.C.U. football players were put to work clearing the Horned Frog field, and at game time snow was banked two feet high around the sidelines. Russell used both substitutes, Harold McClure and Perry Pickett—who later became a District Judge at Midland—in beating Amarillo, 7-6, on a frozen field that turned muddy.

Only Corsicana stood between Masonic Home and a state championship. Because of 225-pound center Richard Kelsey and quarterback Scott McCall—Abner's brother—who weighed 180 pounds, Russell's team had respectable size. The ends were Bill Stages, 175, and Tom Adams, 160. F.W. Wright, 175 pounds, and Allie White, 183, were the tackles. Ragin Gibbs and Leon Pickett were 165-pound guards. Glenn Roberts, 160, was the fullback, and the halfbacks were Reese Newsome, 155, and Bailey Thorpe, 153.

The Corsicana Tigers of Coach John Pierce were no strangers to championship football. In the 1930 semi-finals they lost to Amarillo, and Beaumont beat them in the semi-finals the next year. The 1932 Tigers had scored 313 points to the opposition's 32, while winning nine games and tying two. One tie, with Henry Frnka's Greenville Lions in the quarter-finals, was won by Corsicana on penetrations; the team getting past the opponent's twenty-yard line the most times was considered the winner of tie games in Texas schoolboy football.

Russell wanted to play Corsicana at T.C.U. Stadium, where there was adequate seating; the Masons' crowds were comparable to those at Southwest Conference games. In the regular season, the Masonic Home-Polytechnic contest drew 5,000 fans to La Grave Field on the same day T.C.U. played Hardin-Simmons before 1,000 at Abilene.

Corsicana's negotiators—which included future governor Buford Jester—wanted to play at home, but would come to T.C.U. for 75% of the gate receipts. Russell offered 55%, which was not acceptable. A coin was tossed and Corsicana won; the state championship would be decided there on the day after Christmas.

Preparing for the largest sporting event in Navarro County history, Corsicana officials added new stands to the Tigers' 6,000-seat stadium. Special trains were scheduled from Fort Worth; the round-trip fare was a dollar, and game tickets were a dollar. Snow had covered the Corsicana field, and in the week before the game rain fell almost daily. On Christmas Day the *Star-Telegram* printed directions to Corsicana:

—Masonic Home and School

Several members of the band were also football players, such as Harold McClure, third
from left in the back row, and Glenn Roberts, fourth from left in the next-to-last row.
McClure and Roberts made up half of the T.C.U. starting backfield in the first Cotton
Bowl game ever played.

Highway 34 through Ennis—partially gravel—was the shortest route, but the other—through Dallas' Oak Cliff—was paved all the way. The game would be broadcast over KFJZ right after Lawrence Welk and before Lowell Thomas, *Amos 'n Andy*, Guy Lombardo, and Groucho Marx. In the meantime, Calvin Coolidge was keeping cool in Northampton, Massachusetts, and President-elect Franklin Roosevelt was observing a Hyde Park Christmas.

On the big day Texans swamped Corsicana to see Jack slay the last giant. Spectators packed the stands and spilled onto the playing field. Amos Melton wrote:

> The game here Monday produced almost everything in the way of thrills...the seating capacity of the place was taxed to capacity two hours before game time and by the time of the starting whistle more than 3,000 fans were standing packed about the stadium.

Four times officials stopped the game to clear spectators from the field. A *Star-Telegram* photo showed play continuing while the crowd covered one end of the field out to the forty-yard line. One of the delays to expell fans from the gridiron lasted fifty-five minutes. Near the close of the game an overloaded grandstand collapsed beneath 2,000 fans, but the injuries were surprisingly few.

The Masons and Tigers struggled for the state title in spite of spectators, but neither could score. Three times Mason safety Bailey Thorpe fumbled punts—something he had never done before, even on the frozen field of the Amarillo game. The difference was the crowd: a thousand fans immediately behind Thorpe shouted instructions as he waited and hoped the punt would not carry past him and into the mob. At least one of his fumbles was recovered by Corsicana inside the Masons' twenty-yard line.

When Field Judge Rosco Minton signalled the end of the game the Tigers were on the Masons' one-yard line, but the score was Corsicana—0, Masonic Home—0. Twice before Texas championship games had resulted in ties, and each time the teams were declared co-titlists, but the 1932 game was to be determined by penetrations in case of a tie. Because of the fumbles Corsicana won.

Minton said, "The Masons just didn't have the dash of their other games. They looked tired. The long schedule was just too much for twelve boys to carry." A Dallas businessman suggested a charity game to give Corsicana and Masonic Home a chance to break the tie. The Tigers were receptive, but Rusty Russell's boys had sustained too many injuries to play another game. So the Mighty Mites were undefeated in their first year of Class A football. The standard they set would be maintained through the next decade; in eleven seasons Masonic Home won the Class A district seven times and tied for it once.

Rusty Russell and his Mighty Mites provided an example of courage and perseverance unsurpassed in Texas sport. Allie White—probably the only player to make All-State three times—became an assistant coach at T.C.U., and T.C.U.'s starting backfield in the first Cotton Bowl game ever played was Scott McCall, Glenn Roberts, Harold McClure—all Mighty Mites—and Sweetwater's Slinging Sammy Baugh, probably the greatest college quarterback of the century.

References

Books

Armstrong County Historical Association. *A Collection of Memories*. Hereford, Texas: Pioneer Publishers, 1965.

Army Times, the editors of. *The Yanks Are Coming, The Story of General John J. Pershing*. New York: G. P. Putnam's Sons, 1960.

Bancroft, Hubert Howe. *History of the North Mexican States, Vol. I, (1531-1800)*. San Francisco: A. L. Bancroft and Co., 1884.

Bancroft, Hubert Howe. *The Works of Hubert Howe Bancroft, Vol. 15*. San Francisco: A. L. Bancroft and Co., 1884.

Binion, Charles H. *An Introduction to El Paso's Scenic and Historic Landmarks*. El Paso: Texas Western Press, 1970.

Brann, William Cowper. *The Writings of Brann, The Iconoclast*. New York: Blue Ribbon Books, 1938.

Brown, John Henry. *History of Texas, 1685-1892*. St. Louis: L. E. Daniell, 1893.

Brown, John Henry. *Indian Wars and Pioneers of Texas*. Austin: L. E. Daniell, no date.

Bryant, Keith L., Jr. *Alfalfa Bill Murray*. Norman, Oklahoma: University of Oklahoma Press, 1968.

Carroll, H. Bailey, *et. al. Heroes of Texas*. Waco, Texas: Texian Press, 1966.

Carver, Charles. *Brann and the Iconoclast*. Austin: University of Texas Press, 1957.

Castaneda, Carlos E. *Our Catholic Heritage in Texas, 1519-1936*. Austin: Von Boeckmann-Jones Co., 1936.

Coulter, John, Ed. *The Complete Story of the Galveston Horror*. United Publishers of America, 1900.

Day, A. Grove. *Coronado's Quest*. Berkeley and Los Angeles: University of California Press, 1964.

De Shields, James T. *Cynthia Ann Parker, The Story of Her Capture*. St. Louis: Charles B. Woodward, 1886.

De Shields, James T. *Tall Men With Long Rifles*. San Antonio, Texas: The Naylor Company, 1971.

Dixon, Olive K. *Life of "Billy" Dixon*. Dallas: P. L. Turner Co., 1927.

Douglas, C. L. *Cattle Kings of Texas*. Fort Worth: Branch-Smith, Inc., 1968.

Estergreen, M. Morgan. *Kit Carson, A Portrait in Courage*. Norman: University of Oklahoma Press, 1962.

Farr, Finis. *Black Champion, The Life and Times of Jack Johnson*. Greenwich, Connecticut: Fawcett Publications, 1969.

Folsom-Dickerson, W. E. F. *The White Path*. San Antonio: The Naylor Company, 1965.

Ford, John Salmon. *Rip Ford's Texas*. Ed. Stephen B. Oates. Austin: University of Texas Press, 1967.

Foreman, Grant. *Advancing the Frontier*. Norman, Oklahoma: University of Oklahoma Press, 1933.

Gibson, Arrell. *Oklahoma, A History of Five Centuries*. Norman: Harlow Publishing Corp., 1965.

Gilmore, Al-Tony. *Bad Nigger*. Port Washington, New York: Kennikat Press, 1975.

Gunther, John. *Taken at the Flood, The Story of Albert D. Lasker*. New York: Harper and Brothers, 1960.

Hardin, John Wesley. *The Life of John Wesley Hardin*. Norman: University of Oklahoma Press, 1961.

Haley, J. Evetts. *Charles Goodnight, Cowboy and Plainsman*. Norman: University of Oklahoma Press, 1949.

Halsell, H. H. *Cowboys and Cattlemen*. Nashville: Parthenon Press, 1937.

Hines, Gordon. *Alfalfa Bill, An Intimate Biography*. Oklahoma City: Oklahoma Press, 1932.

Horgan, Paul. *Great River*. New York: Rhinehart and Co., Inc., 1954.

Hughes, Anne E. *The Beginnings of Spanish Settlement in the El Paso District*. El Paso, Texas: Press of El Paso Public Schools, 1935.

Johnson, Frank W. *A History of Texas and Texans*. Chicago and New York: The American Historical Society, 1914.

Johnson, Jack. *Jack Johnson is a Dandy, An Autobiography*. New York: Chelsea House Publishers, 1969.

King Ranch, 100 Years of Ranching. Corpus Christi: *Corpus Christi Caller-Times*, 1953.

Langtry, Lillie. *The Days I Knew*. New York: George H. Doran Co., 1925.

Lardner, John. *White Hopes and Other Tigers*. Philadelphia and New York: J. B. Lippincott Co., 1951.

Lardner, Rex. *The Legendary Champions*. New York: American Heritage Press, 1972.

Lea, Tom. *The King Ranch*. Boston: Little Brown and Co., 1957.

Lloyd, Everett. *Law West of the Pecos, The Story of Judge Roy Bean*. San Antonio: The Naylor Company, 1936.

McCarty, John L. *Maverick Town, The Story of Old Tascosa*. Norman: University of Oklahoma Press, 1946.

McDaniel, Ruel. *Vinegarroon, The Saga of Judge Roy Bean, The Law West of the Pecos*. Kingsport, Tennessee: Southern Publishers, 1936.

McReynolds, Edwin. *Oklahoma: A History of the Sooner State*. Norman: University of Oklahoma Press, 1954.

Maloney, Vance J. *The Story of Comanche Peak*. Glen Rose, Texas: by the author, 1970.

Mason, Herbert, Jr. *The Great Pursuit*. New York: Random House, 1970.

Mayer, Martin. *Madison Avenue, USA*. New York: Harper and Brothers, 1958.

Mayhall, Mildred. *Indian Wars of Texas*. Waco, Texas: Texian Press, 1965.

Mills, W. W. *Forty Years at El Paso, 1859-1898*. El Paso: Carl Hertzog, 1962.

Nye, W. S. *Campfire and Lance*. Norman: University of Oklahoma Press, 1937.

Nordyke, Lewis. *John Wesley Hardin*. New York: William Morrow and Co., 1957.

O'Connor, Richard. *Black Jack Pershing*. Garden City, New York: Doubleday and Co., Inc., 1961.

Paddock, B. B. *Fort Worth and the Texas Northwest*. Chicago: Lewis Publishing Company, 1922.

Palmer, Frederick. *John J. Pershing, General of the Armies*. Harrisburg, Pennsylvania: The Military Service Publishing Co., 1948.

Perry, George Sessions. *The Story of Texas A. and M.* New York: McGraw-Hill, 1951.

Pike, Zebulon. *The Journals of Zebulon Montgomery Pike*. Ed. Donald Jackson. Norman: University of Oklahoma Press, 1966.

Porter, Eugene O. *San Elizario, A History*. Austin: Jenkins Publishing Company, 1973.

Pruiett, Moman. *Moman Pruiett, Criminal Lawyer*. Oklahoma City: Harlow Publishing Corp., 1945.

Randel, Mrs. Ralph (ed.). *A Time to Purpose*. Hereford, Texas: Pioneer Publishers, 1966.

Raymond, Dora Neill. *Captain Lee Hall of Texas*. Norman: University of Oklahoma Press, 1940.
Richardson, Rupert Norval, and Rister, Carl Coke. *The Greater Southwest*. Glendale, California: The Arthur H. Clark Co., 1934.
Rister, Carl Coke. *The Southwestern Frontier, 1865-1881* Cleveland: The Arthur H. Clark Co., 1928.
Samuels, Charles. *The Magnificent Rube, The Life and Gaudy Times of Tex Rickard*. New York: McGraw-Hill Book Co., 1957.
Sonnichsen, C. L. *Pass of the North*. El Paso: Texas Western Press, 1968.
Sonnichsen, C. L. *Roy Bean, Law West of the Pecos*. New York: The Macmillan Co., 1946.
Tilghman, Zoe A. *Quanah, The Eagle of the Comanches*. Oklahoma City: Harlow Publishing Corp., 1938.
Warwick, Mrs. Clyde. *The Randall County Story*. Hereford, Texas: Pioneer Publishers, 1969.
Webb, Walter P. *The Texas Rangers*. Austin: University of Texas Press, 1965.
Weddle, Robert S. *The San Sabá Mission, Spanish Pivot in Texas*. Austin: University of Texas Press, 1964.
Weems, John Edward. *A Weekend in September*. New York: Henry Holt and Co., 1957.
White, Owen. *Out of the Desert, The Historical Romance of El Paso*. El Paso: The McMath Co., 1923.
Williams, J. W. *The Big Ranch Country*. Wichita Falls: Nortex Offset Publications, Inc., 1971.
Wood, James Playsted. *The Story of Advertising*. New York: The Ronald Press, Company, 1958.
Wright, Muriel. *A Guide to the Indian Tribes of Oklahoma*. Norman: University of Oklahoma Press, 1951.

Special Publications

Archambeau, Ernest R. *Old Tascosa, 1886-1888*. Canyon, Texas: Panhandle-Plains Historical Society, 1966.
Brent, Millard Doan. *History of Dodd City, Texas*. Dodd City High School, English IV, April 2, 1959.
Cofer, David Brooks. *Fragments of Early History of Texas A. and M. College*. College Station: Association of Former Students, 1953.
Davis, Albert, Jr. *Galveston's Bulwark Against the Sea (History of the Galveston Sea Wall)*, presentation to Second Annual Conference on Coastal Engineering, Houston, 1961.
Fort Bliss, Texas, Publication of U. S. Army Air Defense Center, undated.
Ousley, Clarence. *History of the Agricultural and Mechanical College of Texas*. Bulletin of the Agricultural and Mechanical College of Texas, Fourth Series, Vol. 6, No. 8, December 1, 1935.
Pliska, Mary Beth. *A Blacksmith's Aeroplane*. Midland, Texas, 1965.
Swanton, John R. *Myths and Tales of the Southeastern Indians*. Washington, D.C.: Smithsonian Institution, Bureau of American Ethnology Bulletin 88, U. S. Government Printing Office, 1929.
Wade, Mary Donelson. *The Alabama Indians of East Texas*. Livingston, Texas: Polk County Enterprise, 1936.

White, Lonnie J., ed. *Old Mobeetie, 1877-1885*. Canyon, Texas: Panhandle-Plains
      Historical Society, 1967.

Magazines

Boggess, Louise. "Brush Eradication on the King Ranch," *The Cattleman*, (July, 1951).
Brite, Luke. "The Bob Fitzsimmons-Peter Maher Fight," *Password, Vol. X, No.
      2*, (Summer, 1965).
Clarke, Mary Whatley. "The Father of Texas Trail Driving," *The Cattleman*, (June, 1955).
Clarke, Mary Whatley. "Scions of Great King Ranch Headed Association," *The
      Cattleman*, (March, 1951).
Cunningham, Joe. "The Last Chief of the Comanches," *The Cattleman*, (February, 1952).
Dillard, Robert L., Jr. "History of Masonic Home and School of Texas," *The Texas
      Freemason*, (July, 1974).
Foreman, Grant. "Journal of Elijah Hicks," *Chronicles of Oklahoma, Vol. XIII, No. 1,
      Section 2*, (March, 1936), pp. 68-99.
Gerald, Rex. "An Introduction to the Missions of the Paso del Norte Area," *Password,
      Vol. XX, No. 2*, (Summer, 1975).
Kyle, E. J. "The King Ranch and Its People," *The Cattleman*, (March, 1941).
"R. J. Kleberg, Jr. Honored by Agricultural Workers," *The Cattleman*, (February, 1941).
"Richard King Honored," *The Cattleman*, (March, 1961).
Orndorf, Helen. "History of Agriculture in the El Paso Valley—The Native Period,"
      Password, Vol. IV, No. 4, (October, 1959), pp. 162-164.
Pattie, June. "Old Blue," *The Cattleman*, (May, 1961).
Smither, Harriet. "The Alabama Indians of Texas," *Southwestern Historical Quarterly,
      Vol. XXVI, No. 2*, (October, 1932), pp. 83-108.
"Texas A & M College System," *The Cattleman*, (May, 1952).
"Texas Ranch and Farm Boys," *The Cattleman*, (March, 1942).
White, Alice. "The Beginning and Development of Irrigation in the El Paso Valley,"
      Password, Vol. II, No. 4, (November, 1957), pp. 106-113.

Newspapers

Daily Oklahoman, October 9, 1956.
Dallas Morning News, October 25, 1910.
El Paso Times, March 10, 1974.
Fort Worth Star-Telegram March 1, 1936; August 29, 1944; June 17, 1962.
The Galveston News, Centennial Edition, April 11, 1942.
Quanah Tribune-Chief, April 19, 1973.
Wichita Falls Record, August 10, 1957.
Wichita Falls Daily Times, February 24, 1946; September 12, 1954; May 3, 1959.

Unpublished Manuscripts

Blake, Robert Neal. "A History of the Catholic Church in El Paso" M.A. thesis,
      University of Texas at El Paso, 1948.
Brashear, Etta A. "Galveston, Past, Present and Future" M.A. thesis, Sam Houston State
      Teachers College, 1941.
Briscoe, Edward Eugene. "Pershing's Chinese Refugees, An Odyssey of the Southwest"

M.A. thesis, Saint Mary's University, 1947.

Cardwell, J. N. "The History of the Development of the Santa Gertrudis Breed of Cattle" M.S. thesis, Texas College of Arts and Industries, 1947.

Casteneda, Carlos Eduardo. "Morfi's History of Texas" Ph. D. dissertation, University of Texas at Austin, 1932.

Chappell, Byron Buford. "Jefferson Davis and His Interests in Texas" M.A. thesis, Texas Tech University, 1941.

Curry, Ora Mae. "The Texan Siege of San Antonio, 1835" M.A. thesis, University of Texas at Austin, 1927.

Davis, Gladys Maude. "The Indians and Indian Campaigns in the Panhandle of Texas" M.A. thesis, University of Colorado, 1937.

De Mauri, Johnnie Mae. "The History of Kenedy County" M.S. thesis, Texas College of Arts and Industries, 1940.

García, José, III. "History of the García Family," 1975.

Garver, Lois. "The Life of Benjamin Rush Milam" M.A. thesis, University of Texas at Austin, 1930.

Harris, Alma Verona. "The Texas Masonic Home and School: A Brief History of the Institution and a Report on the Achievements of Some of its Outstanding Ex-Students" M.A. thesis, Sul Ross State College, 1956.

Israel, T. C. "The History of Oldham County, Texas" M.A. thesis, University of New Mexico, 1934.

Ivey, Rosalie. "A History of Fort Bliss" M.A. thesis, University of Texas at Austin, 1942.

Kinard, Knox. "A History of the Waggoner Ranch" M.A. thesis, University of Texas at Austin, 1941.

Langston, Rosalind. "The Life of Colonel R. T. Milner" M.A. thesis, University of Texas at Austin, 1940.

Lightfoot, Billy B. "The History of Comanche County, Texas to 1920" M.A. thesis, University of Texas at Austin, 1949.

Little, Margaret. "The Salt War" M.S. thesis, East Texas State Teacher's College, 1940.

Perkins, William Coy. "A History of Wheeler County, Texas" M.A. thesis, University of Texas at Austin, 1938.

Phillips, Frances. "The Development of Agriculture in the Panhandle-Plains Region of Texas to 1920" M.A. thesis, West Texas State Teachers College, 1946.

Thompson, William B. "A History of the Alabama and Coushatti Indians" M.A. thesis, Stephen F. Austin State Teachers College, 1947.

Walz, Vina. "History of the El Paso Area, 1680-1692" Ph. D. dissertation, University of New Mexico, 1951.

White, Katherine H. "The Pueblo de Socorro Grant" M.A. thesis, Texas Western College, 1961.

Whiteside, Myrtle. "The Life of Lawrence Sullivan Ross" M.A. thesis, University of Texas at Austin, 1938.

Womack, Margaret. "The Story of a Seawall," 1969.

Ysleta High School History Department, "Ysleta," 1936.

Interviews, Letters, and Maps

Kenedy, Mrs. Elena, Sarita, Texas. Interview with author, October 25, 1975.

Russell, R. N. (Rusty), Brownwood, Texas. Interview with author, September, 1971.

Cypher, John A., Jr., King Ranch, Inc., Kingsville, Texas. Letter to author, March 18, 1975.

Coursey, Clark. *Courthouses of Texas.* Brownwood: Banner Printing Co., 1962.

Notes

1. A New Mexico Rebellion....Castaneda 1936, Hughes, Horgan, Sonnichsen 1968, White, K., White, O.
2. Ysleta is....Ysleta High School History Dept., Gerald, Bancroft, Blake, Hughes, Binion, Walz, White, K.
3. San Miguel chose....Ysleta High School History Dept., Gerald, Bancroft, Blake, Hughes, Binion, Walz, White, K.
4. San Elizario was....Binion, Porter, *Password*, Pike.
5. The San Sabá Mission was....Weddle, Castaneda 1936.
6. The San Sabá Presidio protected....Weddle, Castaneda 1932, Castaneda 1936.
7. Ben Milam led....Brown, Johnson, Carroll, *et. al.*, Garver, Curry, De Shields.
8. Statehood was....Maloney, Foreman, *Chronicles of Oklahoma*.
9. The Alabama and Coushatta settled....Folsom-Dickerson, Thompson, Wade, Swanton, Smither, Wright.
10. Dan Waggoner founded....Halsell, Kinard, Douglas, *Fort Worth Star-Telegram*, Williams, *Wichita Falls Daily Times*, Paddock.
11. Richard King began....*Corpus Christi Caller-Times*, Lea, *The Cattleman*.
12. The Klebergs developed....*Corpus Christi Caller-Times*, Lea, *The Cattleman*, Ousley.
13. The Santa Gertrudis was....Cardwell, Lea, *Corpus Christi Caller-Times*, Cypher.
14. Assault won....Lea, *Corpus Christi Caller-Times*.
15. Mifflin Kenedy was....Ford, Lea, Brown, de Mauri, *Corpus Christi Caller-Times*.
16. El Paso became....Mills, Sonnichsen 1968.
17. A Fort was....Sonnichsen 1968, Ivey, U. S. Army Air Defense Center.
18. Kit Carson took....Davis, Estergreen, Mayhall, Nye.
19. Billy Dixon shot....Dixon, Perkins, *Fort Worth Star-Telegram*, Mayhall.
20. Quanah Parker was....Tilghman, Cunningham, *Fort Worth Star-Telegram*, De Shields 1886, Richardson and Rister, Rister, *Dallas Morning News*, Raymond.
21. Cynthia Ann Parker was....Tilghman, *Wichita Falls Record*, *Daily Oklahoman*, *Wichita Falls Daily Times*, *Quanah Tribune-Chief*.
22. Charlie Goodnight pioneered....Haley, White, L., Archambeau, Armstrong County Historical Assn., Warwick, Clarke, Pattie, Israel.
23. Tascosa was....McCarty, *Panhandle-Plains Historical Review*, Israel, Phillips.
24. The Salt War occurred....Little, Mills, Webb, Sonnichsen 1968, *El Paso Times*, White, O., García.
25. Jefferson Davis was....Ousley, Perry, Chappell.
26. Sul Ross made....Whiteside, Langston, Perry, Haley, Ousley, Paddock, Brown.
27. A & M had....Ousley, Perry, *The Cattleman*, Cofer.
28. Thomas Cree planted....Randel, Day.
29. Dodd City staged....Brent.
30. Roy Bean was....Sonnichsen 1946, Lloyd, McDaniel.
31. Judge Bean hosted....Sonnichsen 1946, Lardner, Lloyd, McDaniel, Brite.
32. Brann was....Carver, Brann.
33. Wes Hardin died....Nordyke, Hardin, Lightfoot.
34. A Storm destroyed....Weems, Brashear, Coulter, *The Galveston News*, Womack.
35. The Galvestonians built....Womack, Davis, Weems, *The Galveston News*, Brashear.
36. Albert Lasker fathered....Gunther, Wood, Mayer.

37.   Jack Johnson was....Gilmore, Farr, Lardner 1951.
38.   "Tex" Rickard matched....Samuels, Johnson, Lardner 1972, 1951.
39.   Moman Pruiett successfully defended....Pruiett.
40.   Lillie Langtry came....Langtry, Lloyd.
41.   Alfalfa Bill Murray designed....Bryant, Hines.
42.   Bill Murray became....Bryant, Hines, McReynolds, Gibson, *The New Republic.*
43.   John Pliska built....Pliska.
44.   Black Jack Pershing led....O'Connor, Palmer, *Army Times,* Mason.
45.   Pershing brought....Briscoe.
46.   Masonic Home was....Harris, Dillard, *The Texas Freemason.*
47.   Rusty Russell's Mighty Mites were....Russell.

Index